The
Moosewood
Cookbook

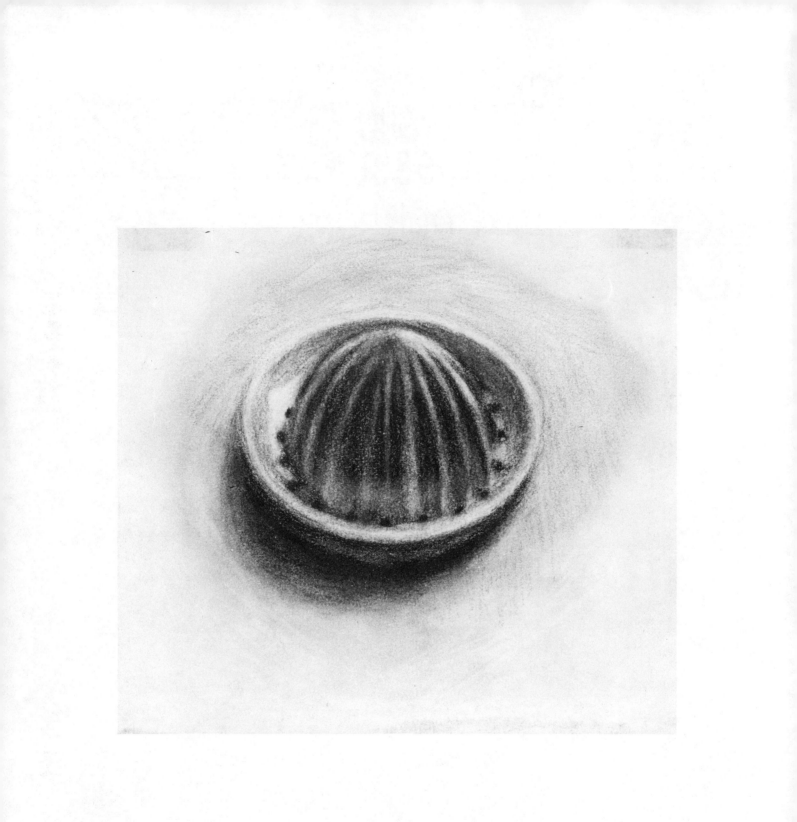

"All wholesome food is caught without a net or a trap." – William Blake

The
Moosewood
Cookbook

Recipes from
Moosewood Restaurant,
Ithaca, New York

Compiled, Edited, Illustrated
and Hand-Lettered
by Mollie Katzen

ISBN 0·913668·68·0 (paper·bound)
ISBN 0·913668·69·9 (cloth·bound)

Ten Speed Press
P.O. Box 7123
Berkeley, California 94707

Frontispiece:
Charcoal Drawing   by Meredith Barchat

Photographs   by J. M. Barringer

Cover Design   by Meredith Barchat
                    and Mollie Katzen

THE MOOSEWOOD PEOPLE,
who have created the
Moosewood Restaurant
in Ithaca, New York,
                    from which
                    this book
                    has sprung:

Joan Adler
Mimi Barchat
Judith Barringer
Marty Blodgett
Linda Brecht
Peter Campbell
Carol Charnow
Jeannie Clark-Fisher
Linda Dickinson
Dilmeran Dunham
Linda Fisher
Andrea Gladstone
Sarah Gowin
Susan Harville
David Hirsch

Cary Joseph
Joshua Katzen
Mollie Katzen
Julie Knie
Tim Lawrence
Stuart Lupescu
Flora Marranca

Lynn Matluck
Nancy McCauley
Patrick McGuire
Kristina Miller
Montana
Kathy Morris
Ira Rabois
Jack Roscoe
Marjorie Ross
Roy Steinberg
Mikel Taylor
Celeste Tischler
Therese Tischler
Mitch Weiss
Frankie Whitman

↑
<u>Moosewood Restaurant</u>
in the Dewitt Building, a
former school, which has been
converted into a miniaturized
community of shops and
dwelling units.
　Ithaca, New York

← The author, Mollie Katzen, in
front of Moosewood Restaurant.

Welcome to the Moosewood Cookbook.

This book presents an adaptation-for-home-use of the cuisine of Moosewood Restaurant, in Ithaca, New York. The ideas for these recipes originated in the homes and imaginations of the many people who cook and have cooked there over the years.

Moosewood is the focal point to which each cook has brought her or his personal culinary heritage from family and friends. (Many grandmothers' recipes are featured.) Cooking styles are shared and traded at the restaurant. Moosewood's cooks also frequent the library, to read about the foods of other cultures. The result is an eclectic cuisine, with vegetarian and ethnic emphases, using the freshest ingredients available.

I was one of the founding members of Moosewood Restaurant, and I cooked there for 4½ years. During that time, in response to customers' requests, I adapted many Moosewood recipes, reducing them to a smaller yield, testing them at home for discriminating friends. Here is a compilation of the results. I hope you enjoy using this book as much as I enjoyed putting it together.

Mollie Katzen
Ithaca, New York 1977

About Moosewood Restaurant:

Moosewood (named after a local maple tree) was begun in September 1972 by a group of friends who enjoyed getting together to cook and eat, and who wanted to engage in a community project. The chosen site was an old brick school building, which was being converted into shops, offices, and dwelling units. It took four months to transform a gymnasium into a ready-to-function restaurant.

After the grand opening in January 1973, more friends of the original seven people joined. Moosewood is now a collectively-owned and worker-managed business with 15 members, who participate in all aspects of running the restaurant, from deciding policy to planning menus to changing lightbulbs. There is no singular owner and no "boss". Any profit that accumulates is distributed among the workers, or recycled back into the restaurant.

The daily menu is posted on large blackboards, as the entrées change with every meal. There are always at least 2 soups, and both fresh fruit and vegetable salad bowls (meals in themselves), as well as 3 to 4 (sometimes more) entrées. Freshly-baked, whole-grain bread (made down the hall, at Somadhara Bakery) is always on hand. Beer and wine, as well as bottled water and fruit juices, are served. Some desserts are sweetened with sugar, others, with honey or real maple syrup. (Moosewood is the only place in town where you can follow up an herbed soybean casserole with a rich, dense, authentically-chocolate fudge brownie.) Every Sunday evening is "ethnic night", with an entire menu— desserts included— devoted exclusively to the cuisine of one country or ethnic group.

There is no specific dogma attached to the Moosewood cuisine. Moosewood cooks prepare meals which are nutritionally-balanced and aesthetically-pleasing, using —in addition to vegetables— cheese, eggs, nuts, beans, grains, bean curd, and fresh fish (served on weekend evenings). Perhaps most of Moosewood's customers are not strict vegetarians (or vegetarians at all), but they are drawn to the restaurant for the experience of a meal cooked with skill and care.

able of ontentment

x

A FEW MISCELLANEOUS BAKED THINGS

DESSERTS

Shopping List

Certain ingredients used frequently in these recipes are not your typical grocery store items. For those of you who are new to this kind of cooking, here is a general checklist to help you equip your pantry.

① TAMARI is soy sauce - good, concentrated soy sauce. It is available in natural foods stores and in oriental food shops. If you can't find it, a good Chinese soy sauce will do.

② TAHINI is a sesame paste used frequently in Middle Eastern dishes. It is high in protein. Buy it at natural foods shops or imported food departments

③ TOFU is soybean curd, resembling a mild-flavored, soft cheese. It is an excellent protein food. Buy it by the pound (usually there are 4 "cakes" to a pound) or in individual cakes, soft or firm. It is available in Asian food shops, and in some supermarkets (in one-pound packages in the produce department).

④ ALFALFA and MUNG BEAN SPROUTS are available in some supermarkets and most natural foods shops. Oriental food places usually carry mung bean and soy sprouts as well. Also, you can buy the seeds or beans and sprout your own. You can do it in jars in your kitchen cupboard .... read the seed package directions. Sprouts are full of nutrients. They have a unique texture and are beautiful to look at.

⑤ NUTS & SEEDS, GRAINS & LEGUMES - Brown rice, millet, bulghar wheat, various beans; raw, unprocessed nuts and seeds - stock up on these at a natural foods store or Whole Grainery. These items are also increasingly available at supermarkets in their rapidly-expanding "health foods" sections. It is strongly recommended that pre-salted, processed seeds and nuts, and white rice not be used in these recipes. The texture and nutritional values for which these dishes have been designed would be largely lost.

⑥ WINES - Keep on hand dry red (Burgundy), white (Chablis or Sauterne) and sherry. These recipes frequently call for wine. As a general rule, you are advised against buying wines labeled "cooking wine." It's a good policy to not cook with a wine which isn't delicious enough to drink by itself. Also, if you are averse to ingesting alchohol, remember that the alchoholic content of wine (or beer) decreases considerably (and sometimes completely) when it cooks. The wine's purpose is _flavor_.

⑦ OILS -   For the recipes in this book, you should have on hand:
    (1) olive oil, for many salads and some cooking
    (2) peanut oil (Planter's is fine) for wok-work
    (3) "vegetable" oil (generic, refined) for deep-frying.
       Unrefined oils are available in health food stores.
They are more nutritious than refined oils, but they are heavier and have influential flavors. It is your option to use them everywhere, _except_ for deep-frying. Unrefined oils have a tendency to froth at high temperatures.

⑧ BLACK MUSHROOMS + TREE EARS
FRESH GINGER ROOT   All of these are available at
BAMBOO SHOOTS   } canned.   Asian food shops.
WATER CHESTNUTS
SESAME OIL - This is not included with the oils, because it is really used more as a seasoning than as an oil. It's flavor is very full and strong. Sometimes you have to take several whiffs to believe anything can smell so exquisite.
DARK VINEGAR
EGG ROLL SKINS

⑨ PASTA · Whole wheat noodles are heavier, chewier, more strongly-flavored. White noodles are more subtle and have much less bulk. They also require less cooking time. Follow your own noodle affinities. If you choose whole wheat or spinach, look for them in natural foods stores, or in very thorough grocery stores.

⑩ Always keep lots of FRESH GARLIC and COOKING ONIONS on hand.

⑪ Herbs and spices are best when fresh. Try growing some indoors. (Easiest = chives and parsley.) But, of course, it is most convenient to buy them dried. Buy small amounts frequently, as they do tend to expire in the heat of the kitchen.

⑫ CHEESES - Please use only pure, real, unprocessed cheese in these recipes and not "cheese products." Real cheese is available in super-markets.

Helpful Tools

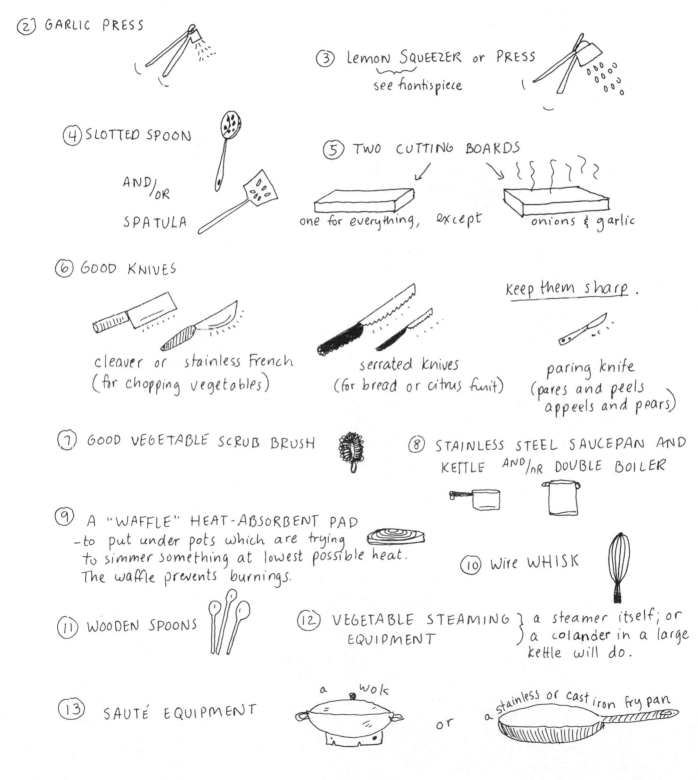

① BLENDER or FOOD PROCESSOR: Highly useful for puréeing (especially soups). If you can't afford these, a food mill, although not an ideal substitute, will do.
   —Food processors are also very handy for making quick pie crusts.

② GARLIC PRESS

③ LEMON SQUEEZER or PRESS
   see frontispiece

④ SLOTTED SPOON

AND/OR

SPATULA

⑤ TWO CUTTING BOARDS

one for everything, except   onions & garlic

⑥ GOOD KNIVES

keep them sharp.

cleaver or stainless French
(for chopping vegetables)

serrated knives
(for bread or citrus fruit)

paring knife
(pares and peels
appeels and pears)

⑦ GOOD VEGETABLE SCRUB BRUSH

⑧ STAINLESS STEEL SAUCEPAN AND KETTLE AND/OR DOUBLE BOILER

⑨ A "WAFFLE" HEAT-ABSORBENT PAD
  —to put under pots which are trying
to simmer something at lowest possible heat.
The waffle prevents burnings.

⑩ WIRE WHISK

⑪ WOODEN SPOONS

⑫ VEGETABLE STEAMING EQUIPMENT } a steamer itself; or a colander in a large kettle will do.

⑬ SAUTÉ EQUIPMENT   a wok   or   a stainless or cast iron fry pan

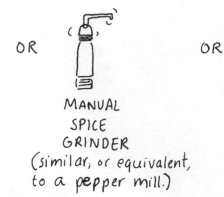

(14) ELECTRIC SPICE
GRINDER
(a little blade whirls
around in a plastic
cup, grinding whole
spices into powder.)

OR

MANUAL
SPICE
GRINDER
(similar, or equivalent,
to a pepper mill.)

OR

Mortar
&
Pestle

—for grinding your own spices and peppercorns. Many of the curry recipes call for ground, fresh spices.

(15) — A kitchen thermometer.
(There are numerous deep-
fried items in this book, which
will come out closer to Perfect
if you know what temperature
your oil is. The recipes will tell
you more.)

(16) A GOOD GRATER,
with many good sides
or attachments, as you will
be needing to grate vegetables,
apples, cheeses and citrus
rinds quite frequently.

Please Note: The "preparation time" message
at the top of most of these
recipes is a suggestion, based
on my own interpretation of the
project. Read each recipe through
before beginning, as you may
disagree with my estimate, and
wish to gauge yourself differently.

Most of the suggestions refer to
the minimum amount of time needed.
Perhaps you are not in a hurry
and wish to savor each slice...
please don't feel you have to
rush to meet the "preparation
time" deadline.

Soups

About Vegetable Stock:

In most of these soup recipes "stock or water" appears on the list of ingredients. You can get delicious soups using plain water as the vehicle, but vegetable stock lends a fuller, more vegetable-y flavor. Stock-making is an old-fashioned approach to soup; it enriches the atmosphere of our modern, expedient kitchens. Further, it makes good use of vegetable scraps which would otherwise be thrown away.

The best vegetable stock comes from discarded skins and innards of:

ONIONS   APPLES

GARLIC   POTATOES   CARROTS   PEARS

PINEAPPLES   MELONS   BELL PEPPERS   ZUCCHINI TIPS

PARSLEY STEMS   TOMATO TOPS & BOTTOMS   PEA PODS

SCALLION TIPS   SPINACH STEMS   EVACUATED CORN COBS

LETTUCE   GREEN BEAN STRINGS   BEET PARTS

If you use cabbage-flavored vegetables or celery, use just a little. Their flavors are too dominant. Eggplant will make it bitter. And don't use citrus rind or banana peels.

Collect your scraps and refrigerate them in plastic bags or tightly-closed containers until you have enough to fill half a kettle. Cover the scraps in the kettle with water, bring to a boil, and simmer, covered, one hour or so. Cool it and strain it. Give it a taste test before using. Occasionally a stock will be bitter, and the bitterness will carry through to the soup.

Cream of Asparagus

4-5 servings

2 cups water or stock
1½ cups chopped onion
6 Tbs. butter
6 Tbs. flour
½-1 tsp. dill weed (to taste)

1½ lbs. fresh asparagus
4 cups scalded milk
1 tsp. salt
white pepper
dash of tamari

Break off the tough asparagus bottoms and discard them. Break off the asparagus tips and set them aside. Chop the stalks, and cook them with the onions in the butter, salting them lightly. After about 8-10 minutes, when onions are clear, sprinkle in the flour. Continue to cook over lowest possible heat (use a "waffle" heat absorber, if you have one) 5-8 minutes. Add water or stock. Cook 8-10 minutes, stirring frequently, until thickened. Purée the sauce bit-by-bit with the milk in the blender. Blend it until thoroughly smooth. Return the purée to a kettle, preferably a double boiler, and add dill, salt, white pepper and tamari. Heat the soup very gently – don't boil it or cook it. As it heats, steam or sauté the asparagus tips until tender, but still very green. Add these, whole, to the soup. ˙Serve as immediately as possible.

Spicy Tomato Soup

1 hour, preparation time   4 servings

1½ cups minced onion

3 cloves crushed garlic

1 Tbs. butter

1 Tbs. olive oil

1 tsp. dill weed

⅛ tsp. (or more) black pepper

[one 2-pound can "Crushed, Concentrated Tomatoes" plus 2 cups stock or water]   OR...   [6 cups chopped canned tomatoes plus their liquid]

1 Tbs. honey

1 Tbs. mayonnaise or sour cream

2 medium, fresh tomatoes, chopped

yogurt, parsley & scallions
   for the topping

Sauté onions and garlic, with salt, in combined olive oil and butter in a kettle or large saucepan. Cook five minutes – until translucent – then add dill, pepper, tomatoes and honey. Cover and simmer at least 45 minutes – low heat.

Five minutes before serving, whisk in mayonnaise or sour cream. Taste to correct seasonings.

Serve hot, topped with yogurt, chopped parsley and scallions.

Gypsy Soup

a spiced and delectable brew of Spanish and Dickensonian origins.

4   servings

This recipe calls for cooked chickpeas. Begin soaking ¾ cup raw chickpeas at least 3½ hours before soup time. (Allow 1½ hours for them to cook.)

3-4 Tbs. olive oil

2 cups chopped onion

2 cloves crushed garlic

2 cups chopped, peeled sweet potatoes or winter squash

½ cup chopped celery

1 cup chopped, fresh tomatoes

¾ cup chopped sweet peppers

1½ cups cooked chickpeas

3 cups stock or water

2 tsp. paprika
1 tsp. turmeric
1 tsp. basil
1 tsp. salt

dash of cinnamon
dash of cayenne
1 bay leaf
1 Tbs. tamari

In a soup kettle or large saucepan sauté onions, garlic, celery and sweet potatoes in olive oil for about five minutes. Add seasonings, except tamari, and the stock or water. Simmer, covered, fifteen minutes. Add remaining vegetables and chickpeas. Simmer another 10 minutes or so - until all the vegetables are as tender as you like them.

Note: The vegetables used in this soup are flexible. Any orange vegetable can be combined with green... For example, peas or green beans could replace the peppers. Carrots can be used instead of, or in addition to the squash or sweet potatoes. Etc.

Cream of Celery

45 -60 minutes,
preparation time.
Plan to serve it immediately

4-6 servings

Bring to a boil in a saucepan. Cook, covered, until soft. Purée in blender. Place in kettle.

{
4 cups celery - in 1" chunks

3 cups potatoes - in 1" chunks

4 cups water

1 tsp. salt
}

1 cup very finely-minced celery

1 cup minced onion

scant $\frac{1}{4}$ tsp. celery seed

$\frac{1}{4}$ tsp. salt

2-3 Tbs. butter

}
Sauté onion with salt in butter until translucent. Add celery and celery seed. Sauté until tender.

Add to first mixture.

whisk into soup, about 10 minutes before serving.

{
1 cup milk

$\frac{1}{4}$ cup sour cream or heavy cream (you can increase this amount for a richer soup)

white pepper to taste
}

Heat the soup <u>gently</u> - using a heat-absorber plate under the kettle, or, a double boiler. Don't cook the soup. Serve as soon as it's hot.

Chili - use chili powder endless

Minestrone

4-6 servings

Note: This recipe calls for cooked pea beans or garbanzo beans (chickpeas). If you use chickpeas, begin soaking them 3½ hours before you make the soup. After 2 soaking hours, cook them in boiling water for about 1½ hours – until comfortably chewable. If you use pea beans, you needn't soak them, but give them 1½-2 hours to cook. In either case, if you cook the beans in plenty of water, save the extra water to use as stock for the soup. You'll have a fuller-flavored, higher-proteined minestrone.

1½ cups cooked pea or garbanzo beans (¾ cup raw)

½ cup dry pasta

1 cup fresh-chopped tomatoes

parmesan cheese

3 Tbs. olive oil
1 cup chopped onion
4-5 cloves crushed garlic
1 cup minced celery
1 cup cubed carrot
1 cup cubed eggplant or zucchini *
1 cup chopped green pepper
2 tsp. salt
¼ tsp. black pepper
1 tsp. oregano
½ cup fresh-chopped parsley

1 tsp. basil

2 cups tomato purée

3½ cups water or stock

3 Tbs. dry red wine

In a soup kettle, sauté garlic and onions in olive oil until they are soft and translucent. Add 1 tsp. salt, carrot, celery and eggplant. (*If you use zucchini, add it with the green pepper.) Mix well. Add oregano, black pepper and basil. Cover and cook over low heat 5-8 minutes. Add green pepper, stock, purée, cooked beans and wine. Cover and simmer 15 minutes. Add tomatoes and remaining salt. Keep at lowest heat until 10 minutes before you plan to serve. Then, heat the soup to a boil, add pasta, and boil gently until pasta is tender. Serve immediately, topped with parsley and parmesan.

7

Hot & Sour Soup

1 hour to prepare   6-8 servings

1 oz. dried black mushrooms
8 cups water
3 Tbs. Chinese rice wine - or dry sherry
½ cup + 1 Tbs. cider vinegar
2 Tbs. tamari
1 ¾ tsp. salt
1 cake (¼ lb.) firm tofu ~ in thin strips
2 Tbs. cornstarch
2 beaten eggs
6 minced scallions
¼ - ½ tsp. finely-ground white pepper

~Chinese sesame oil~
(~ Extra tamari, to taste~)

1) Rinse the mushrooms to clean them. Place in a bowl. Heat 2 (of the 8) cups of water to boiling; pour over the mushrooms. Let it stand at least 30 minutes. (You can assemble your other ingredients in the meantime.) Drain the mushrooms, squeezing out and saving all the excess liquid.

2) Slice mushrooms, discarding stems.

3) Place the remaining 6 cups of water in a large kettle. Add the mushroom-soaking liquid and the sliced mushrooms. Heat to boiling.

4) Add wine or sherry, vinegar, tamari, salt, and tofu strips. Lower the heat, and let it simmer gently about 10 minutes.

5) Place corn starch in a small bowl. Whisk constantly as you gradually add about 3/4 cup of the hot soup. Whisk until smooth. Return to soup, stirring.

6) As the soup gently boils, drizzle in the egg, stirring. Add scallions and pepper. Cook only a few minutes more.

7) Top each serving with a small drizzle of sesame oil.

8

Miso Soup

About 1 hour to prepare
4 servings

Miso is a very concentrated, fermented paste, made from soybeans. It has the same salty taste as tamari sauce, but it is more intense and is always diluted to create the base for Japanese sauces and soups. Miso is a nutritious substance - a source of protein.

There are many different types of Miso, some light (often called "red miso") and some darker. This recipe is adaptable to any kind of Miso. You can check out what is available at your local natural foods or oriental supply shop.

<u>3 Tbs. miso</u> (to taste) dissolved in   <u>6 cups water</u>

sautéed together in a little peanut or soy oil
{
1 cup thinly-sliced carrots

1 cup shredded cabbage

1 cup thinly-sliced celery

½ cup thinly-sliced onion

1 small clove crushed garlic

½ tsp. freshly-grated ginger
}

3 Tbs. dry sherry

2 tsp. dark vinegar

½ tsp. sugar

½ tsp. salt (more, to taste)

lots of fresh black pepper

½ cup thinly-sliced green pepper

FOR ON TOP
½ cup minced scallions
sesame oil
tamari sauce

OPTIONAL
- Extra vegetables (Chinese vegetables, spinach, mushrooms, etc.)
- Chunks of Tofu
- Oriental noodles (soft)

Combine sautéed vegetables and miso mixture. Add sherry and raw green peppers and bring to a boil. Lower heat to simmering point and add remaining ingredients..(except tofu and cooked noodles. Add these just before serving.) Simmer, covered over very low heat, about 10-15 minutes. Pass scallions, sesame oil and tamari to sprinkle on top.

9

Succotash Chowder

Aside from advance preparation of beans, this takes only about 30 minutes to prepare.

4-6 servings

This recipe calls for 2 cups cooked baby lima beans. If you use dry limas, begin soaking 1 cup in water 3½ hours before you plan to assemble the soup. Soak the beans two hours, then cook them approximately one hour, or until just tender. Whether you use frozen beans or dry beans, cook them carefully so they don't get too mushy. That would cancel Charm Number One of this soup, which is the complementary textures of corn and perfectly-done lima beans. So don't, under any circumstances, use canned lima beans! Your soup will resemble library paste.

3 Tbs. butter
2 medium cloves garlic
1½ cups chopped onion
1 cup minced celery
½ tsp. basil
¼ tsp. thyme } more, to taste
1½ tsp. salt
6 cups warmed milk
2 cups cooked baby lima beans (1 cup raw)
2 cups raw corn (fresh or frozen + thawed)
                    (NOT CANNED)
1-2 tsp. tamari
lots of freshly-grated black pepper
freshly chopped parsley and chives

In a large kettle, heat butter and crush the garlic into it. Add a little salt and the chopped onion. Sauté over medium heat, and add celery. Add a little more salt and sauté, stirring, until onions are translucent and the celery tender. Add the corn and cook 5 minutes. Add basil, thyme, milk, tamari and lima beans. Correct seasonings. Let sit, away from heat, until you are ready to heat it for serving. Don't cook it - just heat it gently. Top each serving with parsley and chives.

Cream of Broccoli

4-6 servings
45 minutes to prepare

4 Tbs. butter
1½ cups chopped onion
1 medium green pepper
4 cups chopped broccoli
1 cup broccoli flowerets,
    thinly-sliced
1 tsp. salt (more, to taste)
2½ cups water or stock
2 cups milk
½ cup heavy or sour cream

1 bay leaf
pinch of allspice
black pepper } to taste
white pepper
dash of tamari
dash of thyme } optional,
    or basil   to taste

chopped scallions for the top

optional: ½ cup buttermilk, whisked in
right before serving

Saute the onions in butter with bay leaf* until the onions are translucent. Add the chopped green pepper, chopped broccoli, water or stock, and salt. Cook about 10 minutes, covered (until broccoli is tender, but still bright green.) Pureé little by little with milk, in the blender. Make sure it's pureéd until absolutely smooth. (The texture is very important to the success of this soup.)

* REMOVE BAY LEAF
BEFORE PUREEING

Whisk in the sour cream or heavy cream and the seasonings. Adjust the salt and pepper, if necessary. Steam the broccoli flowerets until just done (again, tender, but full of color.) Combine flowerets with soup in a large double boiler or kettle. Heat gently and serve right away. Whisk in the optional buttermilk as you serve. Top it with minced scallions.

Curried Squash & Mushroom Soup

At least one and
one-half hours
to prepare and
simmer.

4-5
servings

2 medium acorn or butternut squash
2½ cups water or stock
1 cup orange juice
2 Tbs. butter
½ cup chopped onion
1 medium clove crushed garlic
6 oz. mushrooms, sliced
½ tsp. ground cumin
½ tsp. coriander
½ tsp. cinnamon
3/4 tsp. ground ginger
¼ tsp. dry mustard
1¼ tsp. salt
a few dashes cayenne
optional: fresh lemon juice

chopped,
toasted almonds

yogurt

Split the squash lengthwise and bake face-down in a 375° oven on an oiled tray, 30 minutes or until soft. Cool and scoop out the insides. You'll need about 3 cups-worth. Put it in the blender with the water or stock and purée until smooth. Combine in a kettle or saucepan with the orange juice.

Heat the butter in a skillet and add the garlic, onion, salt and spices. Sauté until the onion is very soft. (You may need to add a little water if it sticks.) Add mushrooms, cover, and cook 10 minutes.

Add the sauté to the squash, scraping the skillet well to salvage all the good stuff. Heat everything together very gently. Taste to correct seasoning. You may want more cayenne or salt. And, since this is a fairly sweet soup, you may want to spruce it up with some fresh-squeezed lemon juice.

Serve topped with yogurt and chopped, toasted almonds. (Note: this soup, unlike many others in this book, need not be served immediately. It can simmer a while, and the flavors will mature.)

Swiss Cheese & Onion Soup

1 clove garlic, minced
3 cups thinly-sliced onion
5 Tbs. butter
3 Tbs. flour
2 cups water or stock
1½ cups warmed milk
1½ cups grated swiss cheese

¾ tsp. dry mustard
1 Tbs. dry sherry (or more, to taste)
½ tsp. prepared horseradish
1½ tsp. salt (more, to taste)
black pepper
½ tsp. tamari

a few drops of tabasco sauce
(optional: a dash of worcestershire sauce)

Heat 2 Tbs. butter in a saucepan. Add garlic, onion, mustard and salt. Sauté until tender. Add water. Cover and simmer over low heat.

In a separate saucepan, melt remaining 3 Tbs. butter. Whisk in 3 Tbs. flour and cook, whisking over low heat, one minute. Slip a waffle (heat absorber) under the pan. Add milk. Cook, whisking, until uniform and thick, 5-8 minutes. Add horseradish, sherry, and cheese.

Add cheese sauce to onions and mix thoroughly. Add pepper, tamari, tabasco and worcestershire. Cook over low heat 8-10 minutes, stirring occasionally. Correct seasonings and serve.

Hungarian Mushroom Soup

1 hour to prepare
(approximately)

4 rich servings

12 oz. fresh mushrooms, sliced

2 cups chopped onion

4 Tbs. butter

3 Tbs. flour

1 cup milk

1-2 tsp. dill weed

1 Tbs. Hungarian paprika

1 Tbs. tamari

2 tsp. fresh lemon juice

1 tsp. salt

fresh-ground black pepper (to taste)

¼ cup fresh-chopped parsley

½ cup sour cream

2 cups stock or water

Sauté the onions in 2 Tbs. butter. Salt lightly. A few minutes later add mushrooms, 1 tsp. dill, ½ cup stock or water, tamari and paprika. Cover and simmer 15 minutes.

Melt remaining butter in a large saucepan. Whisk in flour, and cook, whisking, a few minutes. Add milk. Cook, stirring frequently, over low heat about 10 minutes – until thick. Stir in mushroom mixture and remaining stock. Cover and simmer 10-15 minutes. Just before serving add salt, pepper, lemon juice, sour cream and, if desired, extra dill. Serve garnished with parsley.

SUMMER VEGETABLE SOUP

"This soup is subtle and exquisite made with tiny baby vegetables, fresh from the garden, but it can still be delicious in the dead of winter, using whatever produce is available~ and frozen peas and corn."

~Susan Harville~

4-5 servings

About 40 min. to prepare, depending on your chopping speed.

2 large potatoes
1 cup fresh peas
kernels from 2 ears of sweet corn
1½ cups diced onion
2 medium carrots- diced into little cubes
1 cup diced broccoli
1 green pepper, diced
2 little (5-6" long) diced zucchini
3 Tbs. butter
2 cups water
1 quart milk, warmed
1½ tsp. salt (approximately)
¼ tsp. black pepper
fresh thyme (or ½ tsp. dried)
¼ tsp. nutmeg

other possibilities:

snippets of early green beans

summer squash

other possibilities:

a variety of fresh herb snippings (especially basil or marjoram)

Scrub and dice the potatoes. Cook them in 2 cups water until soft. Mash them or purée them in the blender - in either case, include their cooking water.

Add the peas and corn to the potato purée.

Heat the butter in a heavy skillet and cook onions, with salt, 8 minutes. Add other vegetables in order of appearance, sautéeing about 8 minutes after each addition. When all the vegies are tender and brightly-colored add to first mixture.

Slowly add the warm milk to the soup. Add seasonings to taste. Gently heat the soup through (don't <u>cook</u> it; just heat it) and serve immediately - with a good dark rye bread.

VEGETABLE CHOWDER
· · · · · · · · · · ·

6-8 servings

1 hour to prepare.

SAUTÉ in ¼ cup butter:

1 medium onion
1 medium potato, sliced thinly
1 carrot, sliced thinly

salt + pepper   1 stalk fresh broccoli (cut off tough end. Shave
your choice of: tough outer skin from stem & slice stem
  tarragon   thinly. Chop flowerets.)
  basil   ½ lb. fresh mushrooms, sliced
  thyme   1 cup fresh or frozen (not canned) peas
  savory   1 cup fresh or frozen corn
               1 stalk celery, chopped

When veggies are tender, transfer to top of double-boiler kettle. Add 1 quart milk,* ½ pint heavy cream*, 2 Tbs. tamari. [optional: lots of extra black pepper]. If you like, you can add a fresh, chopped tomato. Adjust salt.

Heat over double-boiler just until warm enough to serve.
*If you have the milk and cream at room temperature before you add it to the veggies, this will reduce heating time and lessen your chances of curdling.

Garnish each serving w/ freshly-chopped parsley and scallions. This chowder goes well with crusty, thick slices of garlic bread, especially if the garlic bread is covered with grated Parmesan cheese and broiled for a few minutes.

Best Split Pea Soup

6 servings

Start this early in the day
~ it needs to simmer a long time.

3 cups dry green splits

about 7 cups water
(more, if needed)

1 bay leaf

2 tsp. salt

I.
Simmer, covered,
3-4 hours.

Remove bay leaf.

II.
Sauté in 2 Tbs. oil:

1 cup minced onion

3 cloves crushed garlic

1 cup minced celery

1 small, thinly-sliced potato

2 cups sliced carrots

If necessary,
add a little water to steam.
When tender, add to soup.
Continue simmering.

III.

About 15 minutes before
serving time, add:

$\frac{1}{4}$ cup dry red wine

$\frac{1}{4}$ tsp. dry mustard

$\frac{1}{4}$ tsp. thyme

a few drops of sesame oil

Just before serving
add:

3 Tbs. vinegar

1 cup chopped tomatoes

$\frac{1}{4}$ cup freshly-chopped
parsley

Cream of Spinach Soup

4-6 servings

40 minutes to prepare.

Cover w/ water. Steam until tender. Purée in its own water.
- 1 carrot
- 1 onion
- 1 clove garlic
- 1 potato

Steam 1 lb. spinach in 1 cup water till wilted. Purée.

Make a roux by whisking 1/3 cup flour into 1/3 cup melted butter. Whisk in 2 cups milk and cook over very low heat, stirring, until thickened.

Add the spinach to the roux, along with:
- 1/2 tsp. salt (or more)
- pepper
- 1/2 tsp. basil
- pinch nutmeg
- pinch thyme
- (any fresh herb like parsley or marjoram)

Add first mixture to second. Adjust seasoning and, if too thick, add milk. Heat and stir till smooth, creamy, green, fragrant.

very low flame! ←

ONION SOUP

 (decorative)

4-6 servings

At least one hour to prepare.

5 cups thinly-sliced onions
(don't use red onions)

6 Tbs. butter

1 quart stock or water

1 Tbs. tamari

3 Tbs. dry white wine

½ tsp. dry mustard

dash of thyme

few dashes of white pepper

salt to taste (1-2 tsp.)

optional:

2 small cloves garlic,
crushed

1 tsp. honey

Cook the onions (and optional garlic), lightly-salted, in the butter in a kettle. Cook them until very-but-not-too brown. (Use medium heat to cook them gradually and thoroughly.) Add mustard and thyme. Mix well.

Add remaining ingredients. Cook slowly, covered, at least 30 minutes. Serve topped with croutons* and grated cheese.

* Make your own croutons by sautéeing diced (1-inch cubes) bread (rye or herb breads are great for this) in garlic butter. Spread sautéed cubes on a tray and toast for 15 minutes in a 325° oven.

Cauliflower-Cheese Soup

one hour to prepare.   4·5 servings
Serve right away.

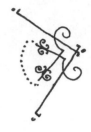

2 cups potato chunks

2 cups cauliflowerets

1 cup chopped carrot

3 medium cloves garlic

1 cup chopped onion

1½ tsp. salt

4 cups water or stock

Place the above ingredients together in a pot. Bring to a boil, cover, and simmer 15 minutes. Let cool 10 minutes. Pureé the entire mixture in the blender until smooth and creamy. Transfer to a kettle (double-boiler, if available) and whisk in:

Heat the soup gently as you whisk these in.

- 1½ cups grated cheddar
- ¾ cup milk
- ¼ tsp. dill weed
- ¼ tsp. ground dill or caraway seed
- ¼ tsp. dry mustard
- black pepper

Steam or sauté in butter 1½ cups more cauliflowerets.
Add these to the soup.
Just before serving whisk in: ¾ cup buttermilk.

Serve topped with chopped scallions and extra cheese.

Mushroom Bisque

Approximately 1½ hours' preparation time. Should be served immediately.

4-6 servings (very rich)

6 Tbs. butter

1 stalk celery

3 fist-sized potatoes

1½ cups chopped onion

1½ cups stock or water

approximately 2 tsp. salt

1½ lbs. fresh mushrooms

¼ tsp. thyme

3 cups milk, scalded

½ pint heavy cream

2-3 Tbs. dry sherry

1-2 Tbs. tamari

fresh black pepper

freshly-chopped chives or scallions

Slice potatoes thinly. Chop celery and mushrooms coarsely. Begin cooking the onion in butter, adding 1 tsp. salt. When the onion becomes translucent add the potatoes and the celery. Continue to cook over fairly low heat, mixing well, so the butter coats everything. After several minutes add the mushrooms, water, and remaining salt. Cover and cook over medium heat 15 minutes. Remove from heat and let cool to room temperature.

Purée the entire mushroom mixture in a blender until absolutely smooth. Return it to a soup kettle (if possible, use a double-boiler or a "waffle" heat-absorbing pad) and heat very slowly, with utmost care, as you whisk in the scalded milk, cream, sherry and tamari. Heat only until hot enough to serve! If cooked or boiled this soup will easily curdle and lose its texture.

Serve immediately, topped with freshly-chopped chives and freshly-grated black pepper. This soup goes well with garlic croutons. (see recipe at the bottom of the Onion Soup page.)

White Bean & Black Olive Soup

(Begin cooking 1 cup dry pea beans 1½ hours before you plan to assemble soup.)

Sauté in

3 Tbs.

olive oil,

beginning

with onions

and garlic.

{
- 3-4 cloves crushed garlic
- 1 heaping cup chopped onion
- ½ cup diced celery
- ½ cup diced carrots
- ½ cup chopped pepper
- 1 cup zucchini chunks
- 1½ tsp. salt (more, to taste)
- black pepper
- 1 tsp. marjoram or oregano
- 1½ tsp. basil
}

Add to:

- 4 cups stock or water
- 3 oz. tomato paste (½ small can)
- ¼ cup dry red wine
- 2 cups cooked (1 cup raw) pea beans
- 1 cup sliced black olives
- 1 Tbs. fresh lemon juice

Simmer, covered, over very low heat – about ½ hour.

Just before serving, add ¼ cup freshly-chopped parsley.

Optional garnish: freshly diced tomato

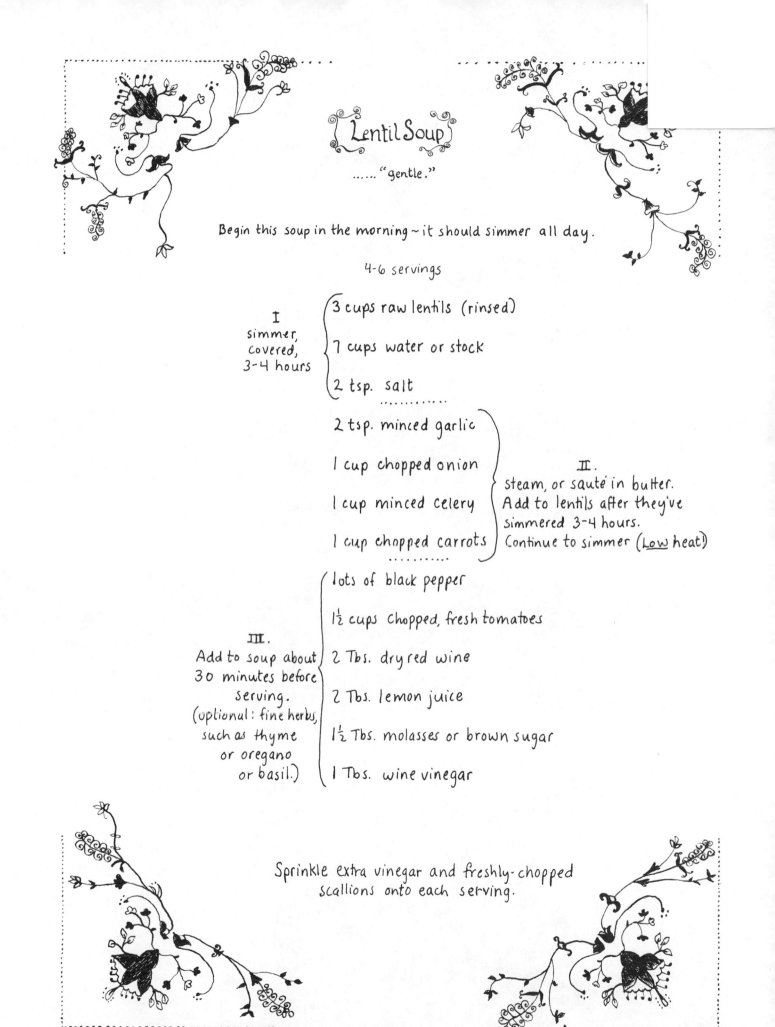

Lentil Soup

...... "gentle."

Begin this soup in the morning ~ it should simmer all day.

4-6 servings

I
simmer,
covered,
3-4 hours
- 3 cups raw lentils (rinsed)
- 7 cups water or stock
- 2 tsp. salt

....

- 2 tsp. minced garlic
- 1 cup chopped onion
- 1 cup minced celery
- 1 cup chopped carrots

II.
steam, or sauté in butter.
Add to lentils after they've
simmered 3-4 hours.
Continue to simmer (<u>Low</u> heat!)

....

III.
Add to soup about
30 minutes before
serving.
(optional: fine herbs,
such as thyme
or oregano
or basil.)
- lots of black pepper
- 1½ cups chopped, fresh tomatoes
- 2 Tbs. dry red wine
- 2 Tbs. lemon juice
- 1½ Tbs. molasses or brown sugar
- 1 Tbs. wine vinegar

Sprinkle extra vinegar and freshly-chopped
scallions onto each serving.

Zucchini Purée

Very easy.
30 minutes'
preparation time.
Serve immediately.

4-6 servings

1½ lbs. zucchini, cut into inch-chunks

1½ Tbs. butter

1 cup finely-minced onion

½ tsp. salt (more, to taste)

black pepper
basil
tarragon
thyme
} modest amounts
(¼ tsp. or less)

2 cups milk, heated but not scalded

1 tsp. tamari

1) Steam the zucchini until just tender. (Steam it <u>over</u>, not in, water)
2) Sauté the onion in butter -with salt- until soft. (5 minutes or so.)
3) Purée all ingredients until smooth -in blender or food processor.
4) Heat gently (don't cook it) just before serving.

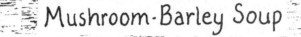

Mushroom·Barley Soup

6-8 servings
1¼ hours to prepare.

½ cup raw pearled barley
6½ cups stock or water

½-1 tsp. salt
3-4 Tbs. tamari
3-4 Tbs. dry sherry
3 Tbs. butter
2 cloves minced garlic
1 heaping cup chopped onion
1 pound fresh mushrooms, sliced
freshly ground black pepper

Cook the barley in 1½ cups of the stock or water until tender. (Cook it right in the soup kettle.) Add the remaining stock or water, tamari and sherry.

Sauté the onions and garlic in butter. When they soften, add mushrooms and ½ tsp. salt. When all is tender add to barley, being sure to include the liquid the vegetables expressed while cooking.

Give it a generous grinding of black pepper and simmer 20 minutes, covered, over the lowest possible heat. Taste to correct seasoning.

Brazilian Black Bean

Begin soaking
beans at least
4 hours
before assembling.

5-6 servings

2 cups dry black beans
3½ cups water or stock
2 tsp. salt

1 hour to prepare
(not including
bean-cooking time)

Ⓐ

1 cup chopped onion
3 cloves crushed garlic
1 large, chopped carrot
1 stalk chopped celery
(optional: 1 cup chopped green pepper)
1 tsp. ground coriander
1½ tsp. ground cumin
(2 Tbs. oil, approximately)

Ⓑ

2 oranges; peeled, sectioned, seeded
½ cup orange juice
1 Tbs. dry sherry
¼ tsp. black pepper
¼ tsp. red pepper
½ tsp. fresh lemon juice

① Rinse the beans. Cover them with water, and
   let them soak several hours. Pour off excess
   water. Place in saucepan with 3½ cups
   water or stock and salt. Bring to a boil,
   cover, simmer 1½ hours over very low heat.

② Sauté group Ⓐ, beginning with onions and garlic. If
   necessary, add a little water to the vegetables to steam
   them along. When everything seems just as it should
   be, add sauté to the beans. Let the soup continue to
   simmer over lowest possible heat.

③ Add group Ⓑ to the soup. Give it a stir, cover, and
   sit down for 10 minutes. Now, return to the soup, refreshed.
   Look at it and ask yourself if this soup suits you. Is it too
   thick? Add water. Do you want it thicker, heartier? You
   can purée some or all of it in the blender. You can make
   it hotter with more red pepper.

Serve topped
with sour cream or yogurt

RUSSIAN CABBAGE BORSCHT

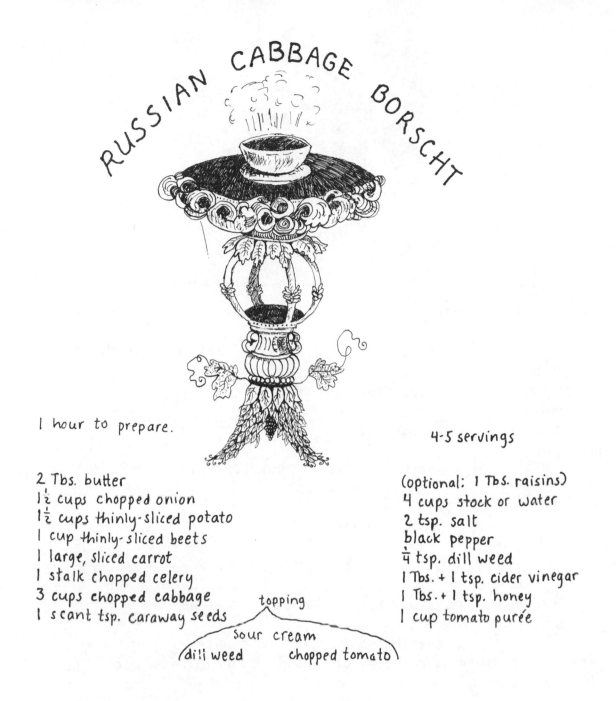

1 hour to prepare.

4-5 servings

2 Tbs. butter
1½ cups chopped onion
1½ cups thinly-sliced potato
1 cup thinly-sliced beets
1 large, sliced carrot
1 stalk chopped celery
3 cups chopped cabbage
1 scant tsp. caraway seeds

(optional: 1 Tbs. raisins)
4 cups stock or water
2 tsp. salt
black pepper
¼ tsp. dill weed
1 Tbs. + 1 tsp. cider vinegar
1 Tbs. + 1 tsp. honey
1 cup tomato purée

topping
sour cream
dill weed   chopped tomato

① Place potatoes, beets and water in a saucepan, and cook until everything is tender. (Save the water.)

② Begin cooking the onions in the butter in a large kettle. Add caraway seeds and salt. Cook until onion is translucent, then add celery, carrots and cabbage. Add water from beets and potatoes and cook, covered until all the vegetables are tender. Add potatoes, beets, and all remaining ingredients.

③ Cover and simmer slowly for at least 30 minutes. Taste to correct seasonings.

④ Serve topped with sour cream, extra dill weed, chopped fresh tomatoes.

27

CARROT SOUP ★★★

"It's the best!" – B. Bunny

45 minutes to prepare.   4-5 servings

Bring to a boil. Cover and simmer 12-15 minutes. Let cool to room temperature.
{
2 lbs. carrots, peeled or scrubbed, and chopped

4 cups stock or water

1½ tsp. salt

optional: 1 medium potato, chopped (for heartier soup)
}

Sauté in 3-4 Tbs. butter with a little salt, until onions are clear.
{
1 cup chopped onion

1-2 small cloves crushed garlic

⅓ cup chopped cashews or almonds
}

Pureé everything together in a blender until smooth. Return the purée to a kettle or double-boiler and whisk in __one__ of the following:

You Choose
{
1 cup milk
1 cup yogurt or buttermilk plus a little honey
½ pint heavy cream
¾ cup sour cream
}
Heat very slowly.

SEASONING COMBINATIONS TO CHOOSE FROM:

| 2 pinches nutmeg
½ tsp. dried mint
dash of cinnamon | ½-1 tsp each { thyme
marjoram
basil | 1 tsp. fresh-grated ginger root, sautéed in butter
plus a dash of sherry, (add just before serving) |

Garnish with grated apple or toasted nuts or yogurt or sour cream.

Cascadilla

15 minutes to prepare   4-6 servings
(It needs, also, to chill.)

~ a chilled, creamy tomato soup ~

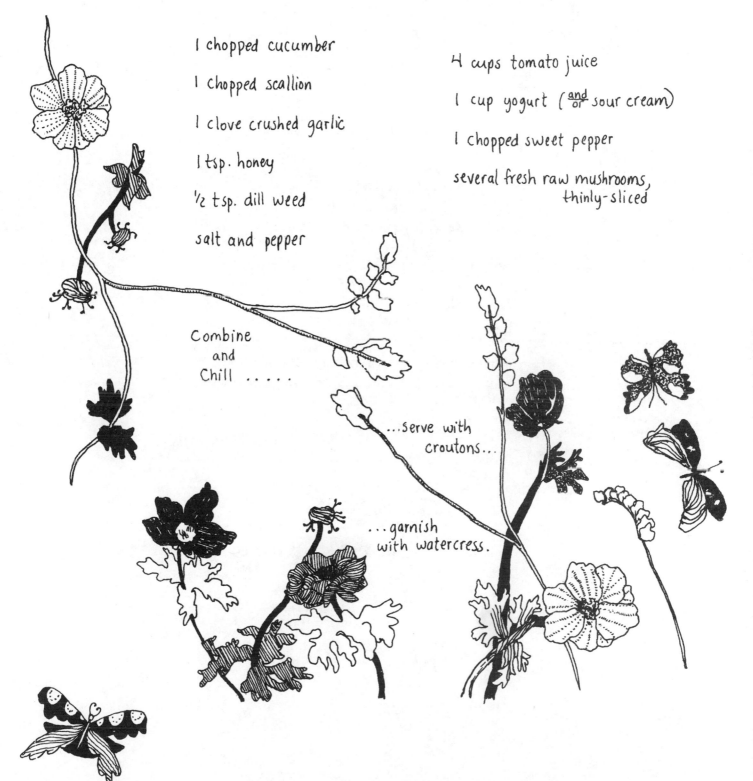

1 chopped cucumber

1 chopped scallion

1 clove crushed garlic

1 tsp. honey

½ tsp. dill weed

salt and pepper

4 cups tomato juice

1 cup yogurt ($\frac{and}{or}$ sour cream)

1 chopped sweet pepper

several fresh raw mushrooms,
           thinly-sliced

Combine
and
Chill . . . . .

...serve with
croutons...

...garnish
with watercress.

Chilled Cucumber-Yogurt Soup

4-6 servings

10-15 minutes
to prepare.
It needs time
to chill.

4 cups peeled, seeded, chopped
cucumber
2 cups water
2 cups yogurt
1 clove garlic
several fresh mint leaves
1 Tbs. honey
1½-2 tsp. salt
¼ tsp. dill weed
chopped scallions or chives

Purée everything together in the blender
(save the scallions for the garnish.)

Serve very cold.

serves 4-6

Gazpacho

20-30 minutes to prepare;   6 servings
2 hours to chill.

4 cups cold tomato juice

1 small, well-minced onion

2 cups freshly-diced tomatoes

1 cup minced green pepper

1 tsp. honey

1 diced cucumber	1 clove crushed garlic	dash of ground cumin
2 scallions, chopped		$\frac{1}{4}$ cup freshly-chopped parsley
juice of $\frac{1}{2}$ lemon + 1 lime		dash of tabasco sauce
2 Tbs. wine vinegar		2 Tbs. olive oil
1 tsp. each < tarragon / basil		salt & black pepper to taste

Combine all ingredients,

and chill for at least 2 hours.

(This soup can be
puréed, if desired)

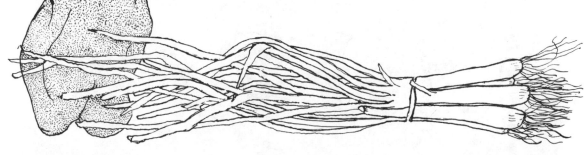

31

Fruit Soup

10 minutes to prepare.   4-6 servings
It needs to chill.

2 notes: ① unlike traditional Scandinavian fruit soups, which are cooked
and contain rich ingredients like onions & garlic & dried fruit,
Moosewood's fruit soups are served chilled and are very light.
② Moosewood serves as many different fruit soups as it has
cooks. Working w/ whole fresh fruits and yogurt and a good
blender, it's hard to miss. So, here is a sample recipe, quite
basic.
        try your own variations.

Combine in blender:

            3 cups fruit juice (unsweetened ~ orange, apple, pineapple,
                                          grape ~ your choice)
        a banana
        chopped, peeled apple
        ½ tsp. dried mint
        juice from 1 lemon
        a chopped, peeled peach
you choose: pieces of fresh cantaloupe
dash of   a couple Tbs. honey   (to taste)
    cinnamon?   1 cup yogurt, sourcream, or buttermilk
    nutmeg?
    allspice?   Thicken w/ more bananas or yogurt if you like
    sweet wine?   it thick.
                Thin it w/ more fruit juice if you like it thin.

        Top each serving w/ yogurt or sourcream
                & a little fresh Mint
                    or a Violet
                    or a Rose

Vichyssoise

~ chilled, creamy potato-onion soup

4-6 servings

Begin this soup
3-4 hours ahead
of serving time,
at least.

1 large onion
¼ cup butter
4 medium potatoes (scrubbed; sliced thinly)
4 cups water
2 cups milk
½ pint heavy cream
1½-2 tsp. salt
fresh pepper
freshly-chopped scallions or chives

1- Brown onions lightly in butter.

2- Combine onions, potatoes, water in kettle.
   Boil till potatoes are very tender. Add salt.

3- Purée. (use all of the water you cooked the vegetables in.)

4- Strain or sieve.

5- Whisk in milk, ½ the cream, and pepper.

6- Heat just to boiling point. DON'T BOIL!

7- Chill until cold.

8- Add remaining cream. Serve topped with scallions
   or chives. (optional topping: tinily-diced fresh red, sweet
      pepper)

Cream
of
Summer
Green

Make this soup at least three hours ahead. It should be thoroughly chilled.

1 lb. fresh spinach
1 small head sweet leaf lettuce
  (approximately 3 cups, chopped)

1 medium zucchini
  (roughly 2 cups, chopped)
1 quart buttermilk
1¼ tsp. salt
lots of freshly-ground black pepper

dash of nutmeg   1 tsp. tamari   1 tsp. basil
½ tsp. dill weed   1 Tbs. dry sherry   (preferably fresh, chopped)
¼ cup each chopped parsley and scallions

Remove the stems from the spinach and steam it in one cup of water five minutes. Chop the zucchini and steam it in one-half cup of water five minutes. Purée both spinach and zucchini thoroughly in their cooking water. Combine in a kettle or large bowl.

Purée the chopped lettuce in 1½-2 cups of the buttermilk. Add to zucchini and spinach mixture. Whisk in remaining buttermilk, and add everything except the scallions and parsley. Chill until very cold.

Serve garnished with parsley and scallions, and pass the pepper grinder around for extra-pepper lovers.

Chilled Buttermilk Soup

4-6 servings

5 thin slices
 Westphalian-style
  pumpernickel bread

½ cup seedless raisins

1 Tbs. honey (more, to taste)

2 tsp. freshly-grated lemon rind

¼ tsp. ground cinnamon

1½ quarts buttermilk

freshly-grated nutmeg

Toast the bread until dry. Cool.

Place the raisins in a small bowl and pour 1 cup boiling water over them. Let them soak for five minutes, then drain off the excess water.

Pulverize the toasted bread in an electric blender and rub the crumbs through a dry sieve.

Combine all ingredients and mix well. Refrigerate until very cold. You can sprinkle very tiny amounts of nutmeg and cinnamon onto each serving as a garnish - along with a sprig of fresh mint.

Chilled Dilled Soup

4-6 servings

Begin this soup at least four hours before you plan to serve it. It needs to cook and then thoroughly chill.

1 cup chopped onion

4 cups sliced raw potato

3 cups water

2 cups milk

1 cup sour cream

1 medium (7") cucumber

1½-2 tsp. salt

fresh black pepper

2-3 Tbs. fresh dill, chopped

freshly-chopped chives
    or scallions

1 - Place onion, potatoes, water and salt in a saucepan. Simmer until potatoes are soft.

2 - Cool above mixture to room temperature. Purée in a blender until very smooth, adding pieces of cucumber as you purée. (Blend all the cucumber in with this mixture.) Whisk in milk.

3 - Whisk in sour cream until uniformly-blended. Add dill and pepper. Chill until very cold.

4 - Taste to correct salt and pepper. Serve topped with chives or scallions.

Note: You can use dried dill weed if you absolutely can't find fresh dill anywhere. Reduce amount to 1½-2 tsp.

Fresh Berry Soup

very easy to prepare   4-6 servings

1 quart fresh orange juice

any combination
to make four cups { yogurt

buttermilk

sour cream

1 Tbs. honey (more, to taste)

2 Tbs. fresh lemon or lime juice

dash of cinnamon

dash of nutmeg

1½ pints fresh berries
(Raspberries, blueberries or strawberries)

Whisk together everything except the berries. Chill thoroughly.
Wash and drain the berries. Blueberries, raspberries or black raspberries
should be left whole. Large strawberries should be sliced. Wild strawberries,
if you are fortunate to have access to some, should be left whole.

When you are ready to serve, divide the berries into individual
serving bowls. Ladle the soup on top. Garnish with sprigs of fresh mint.

Chilled
Buttermilk-
Beet
Borscht

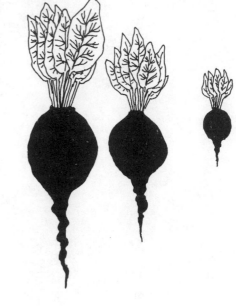

6 servings

45 minutes to prepare;
plus about 2½ hours,
minimum, to chill.

4 large, fresh beets
(3" diameter)

4 cups water

2 tsp. sugar, honey
or orange juice
concentrate

1 tsp. salt (more, to taste)

2 cups buttermilk

fresh black pepper

1 medium cucumber

1 Tbs. fresh, chopped
dill (or, ½ tsp.
dried dill weed)

½ cup very finely-minced
scallions

optional: 1 medium dill pickle,
finely-minced

Peel the beets and quarter them. Place in a saucepan with the water and salt, and cook, covered, for 15 minutes over medium heat. Cool the beets until handle-able. Remove them with a slotted spoon, coarsely grate them, and return them to the cooking water. Add all remaining ingredients, except buttermilk. Mix well. Chill until very cold.

Whisk the buttermilk in before serving. Beet borscht is traditionally garnished with a spoonful of sour cream. Other condiments are chunks of cold boiled potato and chopped hard-cooked egg.

SALADS

A Good Method for Assembling
A Green Leafy Salad

~Use about 2 lbs. of mixed greens for six people.

It's best to use a large wooden bowl for tossed salads. The wood absorbs the oil and flavors and gets seasoned over the years.

The basis for a tossed salad is leafy greens - head lettuce, leaf lettuces and spinach. This method prepares the greens so they stay crisp and the flavors of the herbs and dressing will cling to every leaf.

The Extras of a tossed salad are delicate clippings, shavings and gratings from other vegetables, cheese, nuts and eggs. Prepare the greens first, and have these extras waiting to be mixed in gently just before serving. Make sure, of course, that all ingredients stay cold.

Have the greens washed and patted dry - and all the vegetable trimmings prepared ahead of time. Toss just before you serve.

1- Rub your wooden bowl with an open clove of garlic.

2- Mix together cleaned, dried greens and larger chunks of firm vegetables (NOT TOMATOES!) in the salad bowl.

3- Drizzle in 1-3 Tbs. oil (peanut or safflower, mixed with olive). Toss well until all greens are coated and shiny.

4- Add herbs - fresh ones, if possible. If you use dried, use less. Best are: basil, thyme, dill, chives, tarragon, marjoram, oregano. You don't have to use all of these. And don't be too heavy-handed with the herbs. Toss well after each addition. Add salt and pepper and toss again.

5- Add 2-4 Tbs. vinegar and/or fresh lemon or lime juice, and toss well. Always add vinegar after oil, because oil will only adhere to dry vegetables, and vinegar will wash off the herbs if there's no oil on the greens.

6- Add 2-4 Tbs. yogurt, sour cream or mayonnaise, if you prefer a creamily-dressed salad.

7- Add tomatoes, grated cheese and grated vegetables (carrots and beets, grated, are especially gorgeous.) Toss lightly.

8- Top with chosen garnishes: egg chunks, alfalfa sprouts, radish roses, more grated vegetables, croutons, etc. Serve very cold.

THE RAW VEGETABLE SALAD
. . . .

Dice into ½-inch bits:

carrots

red & green peppers

celery

red & green cabbage

cauliflower

broccoli

zucchini & summer squash

beets (peeled)

cucumber

fresh green beans

spinach or chard

~ any combination, or any
other vegetables: radishes,
scallions, mung bean sprouts,
raw peas or snow peas... etc.
If you use tomatoes or raw
mushrooms, save these for
individual toppings, or they'll
get mushy. Top, also, with
alfalfa sprouts.

. . . .

DRESSING (Yield: 3-4 cups)

1 cup cider or wine vinegar

1 ¾ cups combined olive and
   vegetable oils

1 large clove garlic, crushed

½ tsp. salt (more, to taste)

black pepper

1 tsp. basil

½ tsp. oregano or marjoram

pinch of celery seed

fresh parsley, finely-chopped

juice from 1 lemon
   and 1 orange

optional: avocado
          cucumber
          zucchini
          spinach
            ↓
        (purée right)
         into the
         dressing

½ cup of
tahini
or
yogurt
or
mayo

pinches of:

dill
thyme
dry mustard

Top the salad with toasted
nuts, seeds, or even OATS
(Toast them in the oven)

41

Tabouli

6-8 servings

You should begin to soak the bulghar at least 3 hours before serving time. It needs to thoroughly marinate and chill.

1 cup dry bulghar wheat

$1\frac{1}{2}$ cups boiling water

$1\frac{1}{2}$ tsp. salt

$\frac{1}{4}$ cup fresh lemon and/or lime juice

1 heaping tsp. crushed, fresh garlic

$\frac{1}{2}$ cup chopped scallions (include greens)

$\frac{1}{2}$ tsp. dried mint

$\frac{1}{4}$ cup good olive oil

fresh black pepper

2 medium tomatoes, diced

1 packed cup freshly-chopped parsley

optional: $\frac{1}{2}$ cup cooked chickpeas

$\frac{1}{2}$ cup coarsely-grated carrot

1 chopped green pepper

1 chopped cucumber or summer squash

① Combine bulghar, boiling water and salt in a bowl. Cover and let stand 15-20 minutes, or until bulghar is chewable.

② Add lemon juice, garlic, oil and mint, and mix thoroughly. Refrigerate 2-3 hours.

③ Just before serving add the vegetables and mix gently. Correct seasonings.

Garnish with feta cheese & olives.

Sri Wasano's Infamous Indonesian Rice Salad ☉

Prep. Time: 1 hour, plus
extra time to chill
and marinate

4-6 servings

Set up to
cook:
{ 2 cups brown rice
(cooked in 3 cups water, until tender)

While the rice cooks,
combine in a large
bowl:

⅓ cup peanut oil
3 Tbs. Chinese sesame oil
½ cup orange juice
1 medium clove garlic, crushed
½ tsp. crushed red hot pepper (less, to taste)
2 Tbs. tamari
1 tsp. salt
(optional: 1-2 Tbs. honey or brown sugar)
2 Tbs. cider vinegar
1 cup chopped fresh, ripe, juicy pineapple
(ok to use canned-crushed-in-its-own-juice)

Add the hot
rice to the
bowlful of
dressing.
Mix well,
and
add:

2-3 scallions, minced
1 stalk celery, finely-minced
½ lb. fresh mung bean sprouts
½ cup raisins
½ cup chopped peanuts
½ cup toasted cashew pieces
2 Tbs. sesame seeds
1 cup mixed red & green bell pepper slices
1 cup thinly-sliced water chestnuts
optional: a couple of handsful of
fresh, raw snow peas!

Macedonian Salad

6-8 servings

Begin this salad 3-4 hours before you plan to serve it.
The eggplant needs time to cook, marinate and chill.

marinade:

2 small eggplants	2 cloves crushed garlic
2 medium tomatoes	2 Tbs. dry red wine
2 scallions	juice from 1 lemon
1 cucumber	$\frac{1}{4}$ cup olive oil
1 green pepper	$\frac{1}{4}$ cup safflower oil
1 sweet, red pepper	$\frac{1}{2}$ cup wine vinegar
chopped parsley	$\frac{1}{2}$ tsp. salt (more, to taste)
	black pepper
Yogurt for the top	1 tsp. basil / $\frac{1}{2}$ tsp ⟨ oregano / thyme

① Slice,* peel and lightly salt the eggplant. Let stand 10 minutes.
Broil on an oiled tray until brown on both sides. Don't overcook.
Don't undercook. Slices should be just tender enough so a fork can slide in.

② Prepare marinade. Chop the still-warm eggplant into bite-sized chunks,
cover with marinade and let it absorb as it cools. Chill marinating
eggplant 2 hours.

③ Just before serving, cut the other vegetables into small chunks. Toss
with the eggplant.

Serve on greens, topped with yogurt.

*$\frac{1}{2}$ inch slices

White Rabbit Salad

6 servings

3 cups cottage cheese

2 small apples, chopped

¼ cup raisins

½ cup chopped, toasted nuts

¼ cup toasted sunflower seeds

2 tsp. poppyseeds

1-2 Tbs. honey

juice of ½ lemon

Combine everything

...... serve very cold, on greens

Many optional additions:

fresh, firm pears
peaches
green, seedless grapes
orange sections
cantaloupe
honeydew

extra honey and lemon

45

SPECIAL SALAD DRESSINGS

very easy and good <u>Mayonnaise</u>: (3½ cups)

Beat together in blender
{
½ cup vinegar (you can use part, or all, lemon or lime juice)
1 tsp. honey
½ tsp. salt
1 tsp. tamari
2 whole eggs
2 egg yolks
}

Gradually drizzle in oil while blender is still running.
{ 2½ cups mixed olive and safflower oil } or one, or the other

 The mayonnaise will become thick as the oil is drizzled in. As soon as it is thick, stop beating it (or it will thin again. Strange, but true). Taste to adjust seasonings.

variations:

green mayo ←   → sesame mayo

add ½ cup chopped parsley and/or ½ cup chopped chives

use 2¼ cups safflower oil PLUS ¼ cup sesame oil.

High Protein · Low Calorie Dressing

purée in blender:

¼ tsp. minced garlic
1 cup yogurt or buttermilk
1 cup cottage cheese
1½ tsp. vinegar
½ tsp. salt
black pepper
¼ tsp. dill weed

Bleu Cheese Dressing

purée in blender:

1 large clove crushed garlic
1 cup yogurt
½ cup mayonnaise
¼ cup crumbled bleu cheese
2 Tbs. vinegar or lemon juice
1 tsp. honey
black pepper

 March Hare

a salad invention
which dates
all the way back
to March 1973

6 generous servings

Combine and Chill:

3 cups cottage cheese

2 Tbs. toasted sesame seeds

$\frac{1}{4}$ cup toasted sunflower seeds

diced
very
small
{
1 medium carrot

1 medium tomato

1 fat scallion

1 green pepper

1 stalk celery

1 small cucumber

$\frac{1}{2}$ cup chopped parsley

lots of fresh alfalfa sprouts

juice of $\frac{1}{2}$ lemon

salt and pepper

Optional additions : chopped egg
toasted nuts
chopped black olives

Kristina's Potato Salad

6-8 hearty servings

Scrub 6 <u>medium potatoes</u> and boil them in their skins until they're tender, but not mushy. (You might want to save the water you boiled them in for soup stock.) Drain and cool.

Combine:

☆ The Potatoes, skins & all, diced

☆ 2 chopped, hard-cooked eggs

☆ 2 diced, medium tomatoes

☆ a chopped red or green pepper

☆ 2 minced scallions

☆ a chopped cucumber

☆ chopped, fresh parsley

☆ alfalfa sprouts

☆ ½ cup toasted cashews

☆ ¼ cup, mixed, toasted sunflower and sesame seeds

<u>optional</u>:

☆ carrots - coarsely grated

☆ chopped celery

☆ radishes

☆ other raw, fresh vegetables (peas are great, if available)

⇓   ⇓   ⇓

¾-1 cup mayonnaise (Try making your own. There's a recipe with "Special Salad Dressings.")

1-2 tsp. salt   fresh black pepper

dash of tamari   ½ cup cider vinegar

½ tsp. each ⟨ dry mustard   1 tsp. prepared horseradish
            ⟨ tarragon

Chill well. Serve on fresh spinach with olives and lemon wedges.

48

Perfect Protein Salad

cooked till tender, { ³/₄ cup raw soybeans
cooled. { ³/₄ cup raw rye or wheat berries

marinated in:

salt and pepper
1 tsp. fresh fennel or dill
¼ tsp. dry mustard
½ cup cider vinegar
½ cup mayonnaise
juice of 1 lime (or lemon)
dash of basil
2 Tbs. dry, white wine
½ cup freshly-chopped parsley
2 cloves crushed garlic

While beans and berries are marinated and chilling,
dice:

a scallion
a carrot
a cucumber
a red onion
a pepper
a stalk of celery

Combine everything along with 1 cup cottage cheese and
fresh alfalfa sprouts. Serve garnished with tomato.

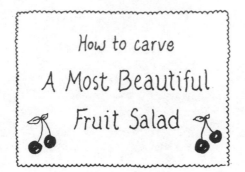

How to carve
A Most Beautiful
Fruit Salad

One of the most celebrated items on Moosewood's menu (and one which is always available, even as the entrées and the seasons of the year revolve, is the Fresh Fruit Salad Bowl. We use whatever fruits are reasonable and available; peak-time, of course, is mid-summer.

Here are some cutting methods for making beautiful bite-sized pieces of common fruits - and for arranging them in such a way as to minimize brown-ness and mushiness. The best fruit salad is one in which each piece of fruit retains its individual integrity. So don't let them sit around, cut, too long, and always mix gently.

ORANGES & GRAPEFRUITS
Use a steel-bladed serrated knife. Cut off the polar ends of skin, then cut down the sides until all the skin and membrane is off. (If you just peel it with thumbs and fingers, it will retain the white kleenex-like stuff under the skin, which looks ugly.)

Using a gentle, sawing motion, cut up the borderline of each section, and out again, releasing the segment of fruit, but leaving the lining behind. You will end up with a fan-like piece of juicy refuse. Squeeze all the excess juice from this tidbit into the fruit bowl, and discard the remains. Meanwhile, you will also have ended up with a bowlful of captivating citrus sections.

CANTALOUPES & HONEYDEWS

Use a stainless steel knife or cleaver. Cut off the polar ends, and shave off the skins, as you did with the citrus fruit. Cut the melon in half after its skin is off, and scoop out all the seeds. Chop it into one-inch cubes.

PINEAPPLE
It's ripe if you can smell it. Again, cut off polar ends and side skins. Again, use stainless steel. Be sure to cut far enough into the pineapple to get all the traces of skin off. Better to lose a little of the goods than to have someone accidentally get a mouthful of thorn.

····· continued ······

Cut the pineapple in half, then in quarters, lengthwise. Cut the center core-strip off from each quarter. This piece of core is unpleasantly hard and unchewable. (People shouldn't have to examine each spoonful of fruit salad before eating it. Fruit salad should serve to help people forget all their wordly cares.) After removing skin and core, cut the pineapple into one-inch pieces.

WATERMELON
The seeds of a watermelon grow in line patterns. Take your chunk of fruit salad-to-be and examine to discover the pattern of seeds. Now, take a teaspoon handle and stick it into the seedline, pulling it along, to evict the seeds. Some people claim it is impossible to remove the seeds from a watermelon (and undesirable -re, it strips the melon of its personality) - but I claim it is an act of love to do this for The Fruit Salad. (If you were just serving a chunk of watermelon by itself, that would be different.) When seeds are mostly gone, chop the watermelon into 2-3 inch pieces. Don't make them too small- they'll disintegrate.

PEACHES AND PLUMS (and nectarines)
Peel peaches only if absolutely necessary. Cut all of peaches, plums and nectarines into moderate-sized slices. Mix in gently.

APPLES AND PEARS
Use only firm apples and pears. Peel only if necessary. Cut into the salad just before serving, or they'll brown. If there's no citrus in this particular batch, squeeze a little lemon juice onto the apples and pears. Without citrus they turn brown and aged before your eyes.

CHERRIES
You can pit and halve cherries and put them in the fruit salad, or leave them whole and put them on top.

BANANAS
Use sliced bananas as a garnish, added just before serving. Don't mix them in, as they'll instantly turn to mush.

BERRIES -
Put them on top only. Cut large ones (strawbs, blacks) in half.

RAISINS AND DRIED FRUIT
On top only. Cut larger dried fruits into thin strips.

TOPPINGS
Cottage cheese, Yogurt, Toasted Nuts and, most heavenly: Fresh Mint Leaves

Tofu Salad

... marinated chunks of
Cloudlike bean curd
(full of protein),

with crunchy vegetables

4-6 servings

If possible, begin
the marinade at
least three hours
before serving time.
(over-night would
be ideal.) The tofu
gains much flavor
this way.

The Marinade:

¼ cup dry sherry or
Chinese Rice Wine

2 Tbs. water   ¼ cup tamari   pinch of ground anise

black pepper   ¼ cup dark vinegar   1 Tbs. sesame oil

2 tsp. sugar   1 large clove crushed garlic   1 Tbs. soy or safflower
                                                                   oil

   Combine all the above ingredients. Cut 5 tofu cakes into
one-inch chunks and spread them in a single layer in a shallow pan.
Pour the marinade over, cover, and refrigerate several hours. Mix it gently
every now and then.

The Vegetables:

1 large carrot   } cut into match-stick pieces

2 stalks celery }

1 cup finely-chopped cabbage   5 large, raw, sliced mushrooms

4 scallions (cut the bottoms into match sticks and chop up the greens)

½ tsp. salt   2 tsp. sesame oil   2 tsp. tamari

juice from ½ lemon   black pepper   2 tsp. sugar

   Toss everything together tenderly. Cover and refrigerate
at least one hour. Combine with tofu just before serving.

Alsatian Cheese Salad

4-6 servings

Toss together very gently.
{
3 cups cut cheese, in julienne strips or half-inch cubes
(combine cheddar, muenster and a good, imported swiss)

1 chopped cucumber

1 chopped sweet bell pepper

1 minced scallion

1 large, chopped, firm, red Tomato
}

Dressing:

juice from 1 medium-sized lemon

juice from 1 large lime

$\frac{1}{4}$ cup mayonnaise

$\frac{1}{2}$ cup yogurt and/or sour cream

$\frac{1}{2}$ tsp. dijon mustard (French-style spicy mustard)

$\frac{1}{2}$ tsp. paprika

$\frac{1}{2}$ tsp. each: tarragon
                          marjoram
                          basil
                          horseradish

Pour the dressing over the combined vegetables and cheese. Chill.

Serve on a bed of fresh greens, with vegetable sticks, pickles, olives and good, fresh bread... A perfect summer lunch.

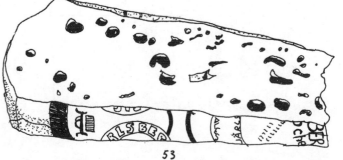

MULTI-BEAN SALAD

Make this one whole day ahead of time.

6-8 servings

This recipe calls for 5 cups of cooked beans. Any kind of beans will do, but it's extra nice if you use several different kinds and one of those is steamed whole green beans. If you are starting from scratch with dry beans, begin soaking them the night before. Don't mix the different kinds of beans until after they are cooked, because cooking times vary. You don't want them too crunchy or too mushy. Cook them in plenty of water (except for the green beans, which should be cooked in as little water as possible.) and test them periodically.   How to gauge amounts: You can safely expect the amount of dried beans to double after they're soaked and cooked.   You can marinate Hot Beans and cool, then chill, them in marinade. They'll <u>really</u> absorb the flavors this way.

<u>The Marinade</u>

Combine all of these.

- ½ cup vinegar (cider or wine)
- ¾ cup mixed olive and safflower oils
- ½-1 tsp. salt
- lots of fresh black pepper
- a few dashes of marjoram or oregano
- ½ tsp. basil
- 3 cloves crushed garlic
- 1 Tbs. dry red wine
- rind and juice from ½ a large lemon

Pour marinade over these and gently mix.

Chill.

- 5 cups cooked beans
- ½ cup chopped scallions
- ½ cup finely-minced red onion
- freshly-chopped parsley

OPTIONS

- grated cheese
- tomatoes
- olives
- eggs

FOR GARNISHES

Carrot-Yogurt Salad

1 lb. carrots - coarsely grated

2 medium apples ~ grated

1 cup firm yogurt

1 Tbs. honey

pinch of celery seed

juice from one small lemon

a few dashes each of salt and pepper

optional variations
{
1 Tbs. toasted sesame seeds

¼ cup toasted sunflower seeds
or almonds or cashews

a handful of raisins

½ cup finely-minced celery

½ cup chopped, fresh pineapple
}

Combine all ingredients, mix well and chill.

Cole Slaw Variation
{ Make cole slaw the same way, but let it sit several hours.

Substitute 4 cups finely-shredded cabbage and 2 large, grated carrots for the 1 lb. of carrots. Increase salt & pepper.

Use half yogurt and half mayonnaise.

Substitute 3 Tbs. vinegar for the lemon juice.

Same optional variations (try using several variations together) and add to your list of choices:
½ cup minced green pepper

½ cup thinly sliced red onion.

Four Waldorf Variations

I. BLUE MOON:

4 medium apples, in chunks
1 stalk chopped celery
¼ cup toasted walnuts (more, if desired)

dressing {
⅓ cup crumbled bleu cheese
½ cup mayonnaise
½ cup yogurt
juice from ½ lemon
honey to taste (approximately 1 Tbs.)

Combine all ingredients. Serve cold, on fresh, crisp greens.
This salad is a good appetizer. It also works well as a
complement to an omelette.

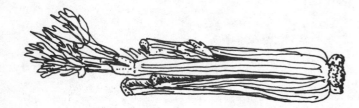 

II. CALIFORNIA WALDORF:

3 large, firm apples, in chunks
juice from 2 lemons
1 large orange (or 2 tangerines)- in sections
1 stalk chopped celery
¼ cup raisins or dried currants
½ cup toasted cashews

dressing {
1 cup yogurt
1 small, ripe avocado (1 cup, mashed)
½ tsp. freshly-grated lemon rind
3-4 Tbs. honey (to taste)

Soak the apple chunks in half the lemon juice. Combine
remaining lemon juice with the dressing ingredients in the
jar of a blender. Purée until very smooth. Toss together
all ingredients with the dressing. Taste to adjust lemon-honey
balance (you might add additional juice or rind). This salad
is a meal in itself.

III. WALDORF DELUXE:

3 large apples, in chunks
¾ cup cubed cheddar or muenster cheese
½ cup chopped dates
¼ cup toasted nuts (more, if desired)
1 stalk chopped celery

dressing
{
juice from ½ lemon
½ cup mayonnaise
¾ cup orange juice
½ tsp. fresh orange rind
}
add honey only if necessary.

Whisk together the dressing ingredients. Toss together all other ingredients. Combine everything and chill. Serve on fresh spinach, with thick slices of whole wheat toast, for a simple and luxurious lunch.

IV. DANISH SALAD:

3 large apples, in chunks
1 cup fresh pineapple chunks
1 stalk chopped celery
1 cup sliced carrot
½ cup thinly-sliced green pepper
1 small orange, sectioned
¼ cup raisins or dried currants

dressing
{
1 cup yogurt
½ cup orange juice (or more, to taste)
juice from ½ lemon
dash of salt
dash each of cinnamon and cardamom
}

½ cup toasted nuts for the top

Combine everything and chill. This salad is a very versatile accompaniment to many of the entrées in this book. It even goes well with Italian dishes, as a refreshing second course.

Marinated Vegetables

Almost any kind of vegetable or bean can be marinated into a pungent, pickled state. Marinated vegetables are delicious as a salad in their own right (try them as a main dish for a summer lunch, topped with feta cheese). They keep up to a week, if refrigerated in a tightly-closed container, and can be used as accompaniments or garnishes on other salads, or as appetizers (see "Italian Antipasto," page after next.) Here is a recipe for a basic marinade, with suggestions for variations. Keep in mind that most vegetables should be steamed until tender before you marinate them. The exceptions are mushrooms, red onions, and salad vegetables (scallions, cucumbers, tomatoes, peppers.) And of course, all beans should be thoroughly cooked before marination.

BASIC MARINADE FOR ABOUT
  3 LBS. STEAMED VEGIES:

1 cup oil (use all or
   part olive oil)
3/4 cup cider or wine vinegar
½-1 tsp. salt
freshly-ground black pepper
2 medium cloves minced garlic
small amounts of herbs:

  marjoram, thyme, basil,
  dill, tarragon, parsley,
  oregano, chives

Choose several. Fresh is best,
  if available.

VARIATIONS:
Substitute part lemon juice
  or wine for the vinegar
  (but don't completely substitute
  vinegar.)

Combine all marinade ingredients
and mix well.
   Add freshly-steamed vegies,
cooked beans (chickpeas are
best) and raw salad stuff in
amounts desired.

Bermuda Salad

6 servings

~marinated fresh, whole green beans and onion slices
with a Touch of Cheese

Marinade

1½ lbs. fresh green beans,
ends snipped off, but
otherwise left-whole

¾ cup good olive oil

¾ cup wine vinegar

¾ tsp. salt

1½ cups thinly-sliced Bermuda
onion - that's the reddish-
purple kind.

lots of fresh, black pepper

2 medium cloves garlic,
crushed

2 cups grated Colby cheese

Red Cabbage Leaves

fresh parsley

① Prepare the marinade. Let it sit while you

② Steam the green beans until tender. Add them, still hot, to
the marinade. Cool.

③ When it's cool, add the onions. Cover and refrigerate at least 3
hours. Toss in the grated cheese just before serving.

④ Serve on a bed of whole red cabbage leaves.

Note: This is a COLOR SALAD.
Don't substitute white onions
or cheese, or you'll lose
the scheme. okay?

Garnish
Lavishly:

eggs

tomatoes

olives.....

sprouts
lemon slices

.... orange slices

Italian Antipasto

Antipasto platters are traditional Italian appetizers, comprised largely of marinated beans and vegetables, complementary to the ensuing pasta course.

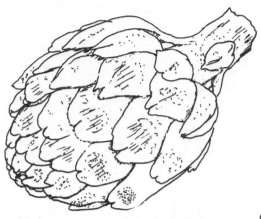

The antipasto can be a meal in itself, if served with bread, cheese, and wine.

Make an antipasto smorgasbord for a dinner party. It's colorful and fun to assemble. And it's easy, because most of the dishes are served cold.

(If you read the "Marinated Vegetables" recipe in this section before reading through this one, you'll get a good, basic idea of what marination involves.)

Make all or some of the following, and arrange them on many little dishes (or on one, large, fresh green leaf-lined platter) for an outstanding salad event:

The Garbanzos

Soak 2 cups garbanzo beans (chick peas, but call them Garbanzo Beans when you're cooking Italian-style.) in water 1½ hours. Drain, place in saucepan, cover with more water and boil until edibly tender (about 1-1½ hours.) While they cook prepare the dressing:

| ¾ cup olive oil / | 1 Tbs. of thin slices of fresh ginger root / | 2 Tbs. red wine |
| ½ cup vinegar / | 3 whole, peeled cloves of garlic / | salt and pepper |

Add freshly cooked, drained garbanzos to the dressing. Mix and chill several hours.

The Cauliflower and The Carrots:

Break a medium cauliflower into small (1-inch) flowerets. Cut two medium carrots into the traditional Carrot Sticks. Steam until tender. Add, still hot to this marinade:

¾ cup olive oil + ¾ cup vinegar + 1 crushed garlic clove + salt and pepper + ¼ cup grated parmesan cheese. Mix and chill.

The Mushrooms:

Clean ½ lb. medium-sized mushrooms and remove the stems. (Set the stems aside for some other use – soup or sauce.) Steam the caps five minutes, them marinate them in the following:

½ cup olive oil, 2 Tbs. dry white wine, ¼ cup fresh lemon juice, ¼ cup freshly-chopped parsley, ¼ cup finely-minced scallions or chives, ½ tsp. thyme, 1 clove crushed garlic, salt and pepper.

Mix well and chill several hours.

The Swiss Chard:

Coarsely chop 1 lb. fresh swiss chard. Thinly-slice one medium white onion. Heat 3 Tbs. olive oil in a heavy skillet. Add onions, a little salt, a few pinches of oregano. Sauté until onion is soft and translucent. Add chopped chard and stir-fry until the chard is wilted and deep, deep green. Remove from heat. Toss with 3 Tbs. vinegar, add salt and pepper to taste. Serve hot or cold.

The Peppers:

Cut 4 or 5 large green and red bell peppers into strips. Sauté in 2 Tbs. butter and 2 Tbs. olive oil with 1 small clove crushed garlic. Add salt and pepper to taste. Serve hot or room temperature.

The Artichokes:

Cook 4 large artichokes in water 40 minutes or so (in the usual fashion) until done. Split each artichoke in half lengthwise and marinate, face-down, in a shallow pan in:

¼ cup fresh lemon juice, ½ cup olive oil, 1 tsp. tarragon, 1 clove crushed garlic, salt and pepper.

Baste them as they marinate.

Other Items:

~Hard-boiled egg halves, with a dollop of sour cream & a sprinkling of chives   ~ All kinds of fresh, raw vegetable sticks   ~exotic olives
~ Good, fresh bread and blocks of good cheese.

Balkan Cucumber Salad

4-6 servings

15-20 minutes,
preparation time

4 medium (7-inch) cucumbers

3/4 cup sour cream

3/4 cup yogurt

2 small cloves crushed garlic

4 fresh mint leaves, minced

½ cup very thinly-sliced
    red onion
(Don't use any other kind
  of onion. Red is the
  only kind that works
  raw this way)

¼ cup very-finely-chopped parsley

¼ cup minced scallion greens

optional: 1-2 tsp. honey

1 tsp. salt

lots of black pepper

1 Tbs. freshly-chopped dill
  (or- 1 tsp. dried)

1 cup chopped toasted walnuts

Peel and slice the cucumbers (unless they're home-grown and unwaxed, in which case, don't peel them.) Combine all ingredients except walnuts. Chill thoroughly and serve on a bed of fresh, crisp greens, with walnuts on top. Garnish lavishly with:
* HARD-COOKED EGG SLICES *
* TOMATO WEDGES *
* CHOPPED BLACK OLIVES *
* CARROT SLICES *

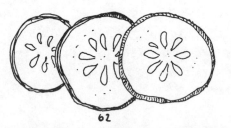

SAUCES, SANDWICHES AND SPREADS

"Sauces, Sandwiches and Spreads" OR "How to Take plain cooked rice or beans or vegetables or a hunk of plain bread and make it into a complete and interesting meal by concocting something nutritious and exotic to pour over it or spread on it or dunk it into."

Examples (just a very few of the many possibilities):

→ Asparagus-Mushroom Sauce on plain, cooked spaghetti

→ Cashew-Ginger Sauce on plain, cooked grains

→ Aioli on hard-boiled eggs and steamed vegetables

→ Spinach-Yogurt Sauce on poached eggs & baked potatoes

→ A Bowlful of Humus, surrounded by raw vegetables and fresh pita bread (recipe for pita in "Miscellaneous Baked Things" chapter) — a surprisingly filling meal.

→ Etcetera.

You can also use many of these ideas for appetizers or toppings for baked fish. For those of you who have been too shy to innovate in the kitchen, perhaps this chapter will encourage you to experiment with new combinations.

Lovely Sesame Sauce

$\frac{1}{4}$ cup butter

$\frac{1}{4}$ cup flour

$\frac{1}{2}$ tsp. salt

$\frac{1}{4}$ cup minced onion

1 clove crushed garlic

$\frac{1}{2}$ cup tahini

room temperature { 1$\frac{1}{2}$ cups orange juice

1 cup water

1 Tbs. tamari

1 tsp. honey

1) Melt butter in a saucepan over low heat. Add onion, garlic and salt. Cook slowly for about 5 minutes, or until onion is translucent. Whisk in flour. Cook, whisking, 5 minutes.

2) Add tahini. Continue to cook over lowest heat, whisking frequently.

3) Add remaining ingredients. Simmer very gently 10 minutes.

Best on { Baked eggplant / Sautéed vegetables / Baked fish / Your favorite grains }, about 5 servings' coverage.

Italian Tomato Sauce

This recipe makes plenty for a big pan of Lasagne or Parmesan.

🍅 SAUTÉ IN A LARGE KETTLE:

  3 Tbs. olive oil
  1 cup chopped onion
  1 Tbs. minced garlic
  1 cup chopped green pepper
  2 tsp. basil
  1 tsp. oregano
  2 bay leaves
  2 tsp. salt

🍅 WHEN ONIONS ARE CLEAR AND VERY SOFT, ADD:

  1 1lb.-13 oz. can tomato purée
  1 6-oz. can tomato paste
  2 Tbs. dry red wine
  1 cup freshly-chopped tomatoes
  $\frac{1}{4}$ tsp. black pepper

🍅 TURN THE HEAT WAY DOWN. COVER AND SIMMER
AT LEAST 45 MINUTES, STIRRING OCCASIONALLY. THEN ADD:

  $\frac{1}{2}$ cup freshly-chopped parsley
  (if necessary, more salt and pepper)

OPTIONAL: ····$\frac{1}{2}$ lb. coarsely-chopped mushrooms
                    (sautéed with step 1)

              ····$\frac{1}{2}$ cup grated parmesan or romano
                    (add last)

asparagus~mushroom sauce

enough for 4-6 platesful of pasta
also good on rice or fish

3/4-1 lb. chopped mushrooms
1½ cups water
milk (approximately ½-3/4 cup)
1 cup chopped onion
1 clove crushed garlic (or more)
2 cups thinly, diagonally-cut asparagus
4 Tbs. butter
4 Tbs. flour
½ tsp. tarragon
salt and pepper to taste (tamari is optional)

optional topping:
   grated parmesan

① Salt the mushrooms lightly and steam them 10 minutes in the water. Drain and press out all excess liquid. Measure the liquid, and add enough milk to make 3 cups.
② Cook the asparagus in a steamer 10 minutes or so (until it is the consistency you like.)
③ Melt butter. Add onions and garlic. When onions become soft, whisk in the flour. Cook, whisking over low heat 5 minutes. Add liquid from ①. Cook, stirring frequently, until it thickens (low heat, 8-10 minutes.) Add mushrooms and asparagus. Season to taste.

(make this right
before serving, or
it'll lose its color)

spinach-yogurt sauce

4 servings

Good on grains, noodles (add some parmesan); baked potatoes, poached eggs

1 lb. fresh spinach - cleaned and stemmed
½ tsp. salt
1 cup firm yogurt, room temperature
2 Tbs. sour cream
2 Tbs. butter
2 Tbs. flour
black pepper to taste
pinch of nutmeg

optional: ½ cup chopped onions,
            sautéed in butter

            ½ cup grated cheddar

Place wet, washed spinach in a saucepan, add salt, and cook until just slightly pooped and very deep green. Purée the cooked spinach in its own liquid, in a blender.

Melt butter. Whisk in flour. Cook, whisking 2-3 minutes. Add spinach purée and cook 5 minutes, stirring frequently. Add seasonings (and onions and/or cheese). Just before serving whisk in the yogurt and sour cream.

Egg Sauce ooooo

3 Tbs. butter
3 Tbs. flour
2 Hard-boiled eggs } puréed together
1½ cups milk   }   in blender
¼ tsp. dry mustard
salt and white pepper to taste
¼ tsp. horseradish (prepared)

optional: a dash of finely-minced garlic
          fresh chives and parsley

① Melt butter. Whisk in flour. Lower heat and cook, whisking 2 minutes.

② Whisk in puréed milk and egg mixture, plus the seasonings. Simmer
8-10 minutes, whisking frequently.

This sauce is a superlative experience on baked fish (makes enough
to cover four servings), It is also good on steamed, fresh vegetables
and potatoes.

Cashew-Ginger Sauce

Puree until very smooth in blender. Heat gently. Stir from the bottom as you serve.

{
2 cups toasted cashew pieces (use plain, unsalted cashews and toast them in your broiler)
3 cups water or milk
2 tsp. freshly-grated ginger
2 tsp. tamari } more, to taste
½ tsp. salt
}

If you want a thicker, creamier sauce that goes a little further, make a roux:

Melt ~ 3 Tbs. butter
whisk in ~ 3 Tbs. flour.

Cook, whisking over low heat 2-5 minutes. Whisk in heated cashew purée, and cook an additional 8-10 minutes.

Serve over steamed or sautéed vegetables and/or grains. Top with chopped scallions.

— —

MONDO BIZZARO SAUCE

~ for your Spaghetti ~

(jazzy pesto)

purée in blender

4 cloves garlic

10 leaves fresh basil (or 2 Tbs. dried)

2 cups tomato purée

½ lb. fresh, chopped spinach leaves

½ cup chopped parsley

¾ cup olive oil

¾ cup freshly-grated Parmesan or Romano

heat gently and toss with hot pasta

You can buy delicious duck or plum sauce in oriental food stores, but it is more rewarding to make your own. This recipe makes more than enough for 2 4-person bouts with Vegetarian Eggrolls, or several episodes of Indonesian Rice Salad (see the recipe in "Salads" section.) It keeps very well (several weeks) if stored in a sterile, air-tight container under refrigeration.

5 cups (heaping, even) mixed apples, peaches, pears and plums (FRESH ONLY!) - skinned & chopped

1 cup water

¼ cup cider vinegar

¼ cup brown sugar (light is better for this than dark)

¼ tsp. salt

2 tsp. tamari

1 clove (medium-sized) garlic, crushed

Combine everything in a heavy sauce pan and bring to a boil. Turn the heat down and simmer, uncovered until all the fruit is tender (about ½ hour). Cool thoroughly before serving.

You can leave it in chunky form, or take a masher to it lightly. Don't purée or strain it, or it will acquire the dubious texture of baby food.

Aioli

garlic-mayonnaise sauce

The traditional aioli supper consists of the central dish ~ garlic-mayonnaise~ and surrounding clusters of freshly-steamed vegetables to dip. Serve these on a bed of fresh spinach, accompanied by chunks of hard-cooked eggs, tomatoes and good bread. The best vegetables to steam for aioli are green beans, potatoes, broccoli, cauliflower, mushrooms, and strips of carrot.

Aioli is also delicious on freshly-baked fish. Bake the fish in just a little lemon juice, butter, salt and pepper. Spread the room-temperature mayonnaise onto the hot fish. Sprinkle with minced chives or scallions.

This recipe makes enough for an aioli supper for 4 people. It will amply cover four servings of fish, if that's what you're planning, and there should be some extra for dipping potatoes or whatever you're serving with the fish. This only takes about 10 minutes to prepare.

combine these in a blender. Blend well.
{
½ cup fresh-squeezed lemon juice
½ tsp. salt
1 tsp. tamari
3 medium cloves crushed garlic
2 whole eggs
2 egg yolks
}

2½ cups oil (use all or part olive oil.)

After blending the first six ingredients thoroughly at high speed, turn the blender speed down to medium. Gradually drizzle in the oil. Don't just dump it in all at once. Keep the blender running at medium until all the oil is entered. The mixture should be thick. Once it's thick, turn the blender off. Mayonnaise has strange ways - if you beat it too long it will get thin again, which, of course, you don't want to happen.

Raita

The authentic way to serve a curry involves many condiments, ranging from toasted nuts or coconut, slices of fresh fruit and vegetables, to raisins, chutney and yogurt. A raita is basically a yogurt dish, with the addition of just a few light touches of spice and a featured fruit or vegetable. Raita is a mouth-cooler - the perfect complement to spiciness.

Here are two basic Raitas:

Cucumber Raita

(Each serves about six)

Banana Raita

1 medium cucumber (7-inch)

3 cups yogurt

1 tsp. cumin seed

1 tsp. salt

dash of cayenne

2 bananas - ripe, but not over-ripe

3 cups yogurt

dash of cayenne

dash of cinnamon

dash of cardamom

1 tsp. fresh lemon juice

Peel, seed, and coarsely grate the cucumber.

Roast the whole cumin seeds in a heavy skillet, or under the broiler for about 5 minutes. Grind them in a spice-grinder or mortar and pestle. Combine everything and chill.

Garnish with fresh mint leaves.

Purée one of the bananas in a blender, with some of the yogurt. Chop the other banana into ½-inch chunks.

Combine all ingredients and chill.

CHUTNEY

... The mysterious Indian relish, demystified. It's only slightly more complicated to make than applesauce. And you can vary its sweetness, non-sweetness or relative spiciness according to your own taste.

Preparation time should include an hour to simmer and several hours (or even days) to ripen. Chutney will keep, if packaged in a sterile, sealed jar. Each of these recipes makes in the neighborhood of a quart.

APPLE CHUTNEY

1½ lbs. cooking apples
 (You can also use combinations
   of peaches and pears.)
1 medium clove garlic, minced
1 Tbs. chopped ginger root
½ cup orange juice
1 tsp. cinnamon
1 tsp. cloves
1 tsp. salt
1 cup honey (more to taste)
1 cup cider vinegar
cayenne to taste

Coarsely chop the apples. (You needn't peel them.)

Combine everything in a heavy saucepan. Bring to a boil, then lower to a simmer.

Simmer, uncovered, stirring occasionally, 45 minutes - 1 hour. Cool before storing in a jar.

GREEN TOMATO CHUTNEY

2 lbs. green tomatoes
2 Tbs. freshly-chopped ginger
2 cloves minced garlic
½ tsp. mustard seeds
1 tsp. ground cumin
1 tsp. ground coriander
2 tsp. salt
1 cup honey
1 cup cider vinegar
cayenne to taste

Chop the tomatoes.

Combine everything. Bring to a boil, then simmer one hour, stirring now and then.

Cool before packing.

Pesto

~ for about six servings of pasta or Gnocchi.

3 packed cups fresh basil leaves
    (removed from stems)

2 large cloves fresh garlic

½ cup pine nuts, walnuts, almonds
    or a combination

3/4 cup (packed) fresh-chopped parsley

3/4 cup fresh-grated parmesan

½ cup olive oil

¼ cup melted butter

salt to taste

Combine everything in a blender on low, then medium speed. (Arrange things so the blender blade will turn efficiently.) Thoroughly work everything into a smooth paste. Toss with hot, drained pasta or spoon onto hot Gnocchi.

. . . .

Pesto is a potent green paste, featuring fresh basil leaves. (Dried basil will <u>not</u> do.) Because basil is easier to grow out-of-doors than in a pot, the pesto season is limited to late summer in upstate New York. Because of this limitation, its specialness is augmented.

Pesto is also rich in protein (nuts and cheese).

Tahini-Lemon Sauce

This recipe makes plenty of sauce for 6 servings of Felafel (in "Entrées" chapter). You can also serve it with sautéed vegetables - especially eggplant. Another possibility is to slightly increase the ratio of yogurt or buttermilk to tahini and use it as a hearty salad dressing. This takes only a few minutes to prepare.

1½ cups tahini

1½ cups yogurt
or buttermilk

1 medium clove crushed garlic

½ cup fresh-squeezed lemon juice

¼ cup finely-minced scallions

¼ cup finely-minced parsley

salt to taste

dash or two of cayenne

dash or two of paprika

½ tsp. ground cumin
(more, to taste)

dash or two of tamari

Beat well, using a whisk, wooden spoon or even electric mixer. (The more you whip it, the thicker it becomes. Follow your own personal designs)

Serve room temperature on hot felafel or vegetables.

Serve chilled on salad.

Nachos Sauce

Give this sauce
several hours
to simmer.

4 servings

This is a Mexican beer-cheese sauce.

It is very rich, and could turn plain beans and rice into a very special (and filling) meal. It is delicious enough to dip plain, steamed tortillas in – and call it Lunch.

1½ cups chopped onion
3 medium cloves crushed garlic
¼ cup olive oil
¼ cup whole wheat flour
½ tsp. ground cumin
½ tsp. ground coriander
¼ tsp. cayenne
1 large, chopped bell pepper
2 medium chopped tomatoes
2 cups grated mild, white cheese
   (Brick or Monterey Jack)
1 tsp. salt
¼ tsp. black pepper
12 oz. beer or ale (room temperature)
2 tsp. sugar

In a saucepan:

Sauté onion and garlic in olive oil with salt and spices. When onion is translucent add peppers and tomatoes. Sauté 10 minutes more, then sprinkle in the flour. Stir and cook about 5-8 minutes, then add the beer. Cook over medium heat, stirring frequently, 15 minutes. Then turn the heat way down, cover it, and let it simmer at least an hour – coming back for a good stir every 15 or so minutes. If possible, let the Nachos simmer several hours. Then sprinkle in the sugar, remove from the heat, uncover, and let stand about 45 minutes.

Heat gently to serve, sprinkling in the cheese as it heats. Serve very hot.

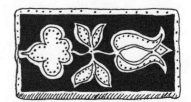

Salsa Yucateco

About 25 minutes,
preparation time

Enough to cover
4 servings
of fish or rice

This recipe comes from the Yucatan area of Mexico. It was designed for baked fish, but it is also delicious on plain, cooked rice.

You will notice a strange spice - "achiote seed" (also called "annatto" in some places.) It has a very mild flavor and a beautiful red color. If you can't find it in exotic spice stores, substitute a mild paprika.

1½ cups diced onion
½ cup chopped green olives
  & pimientos
1 large green pepper, minced
¼ cup olive oil
juice from 1 large lemon
1 Tbs. ground achiote seed
  (make sure you grind it
   very fine. Use a spice
   grinder, blender, or
   mortar & pestle.)
1 tsp. ground coriander
1 cup fresh orange juice
salt and black pepper

In a large, heavy skillet, saute onion in the olive oil until translucent. Add chopped olives and peppers. Sauté 5 minutes.

Add all other ingredients and simmer 5-8 minutes. If you are going to use this sauce for fish, bake the fish right in it. If you plan to serve it as a topping for rice, ladle it onto cooked rice (don't cook them together.)

Serve with a salad of diced cucumbers, scallions and tomatoes in olive oil and vinegar (tossed with a few whole, roasted cumin seeds.)

77

MEXICAN HOT SAUCE

1 cup chopped onion

2 cloves crushed garlic

3 cups chopped tomatoes *

1 cup water

1 tsp. salt

1 tsp. cumin

$\frac{1}{4}$ tsp. ground coriander

2 tsp. dry red wine

*you can use red
or green tomatoes

$\frac{1}{4}$ - $\frac{1}{2}$ tsp. cayenne

$\frac{1}{4}$ tsp. black pepper

$\frac{1}{2}$ tsp. chili powder

2 Tbs. tomato paste

2 Tbs. olive oil

Sauté onions and garlic in olive oil with $\frac{1}{2}$ tsp. salt until onion is clear. Add spices. Transfer to saucepan and add tomatoes, water, tomato paste and wine. Add remaining salt. Cover and simmer $\frac{1}{2}$ hour, or longer. Several hours is best.

Hot spices tend to get hotter as they cook. It is recommended that you add the cayenne a little at a time, so the degree of hotness is to your tolerance.

This sauce can be left in chunky form. Or, you can purée all or part of it.

Sour cream-horseradish sauce

2 egg yolks

1 cup sour cream

1 Tbs. horseradish

juice from 1 lemon

½ tsp. salt

dash of sugar

¼ cup minced scallions (garnish)

whisk egg yolks into sour cream.

Add other ingredients.

Heat very slowly over a double boiler, whisking periodically. 8-10 minutes.

This recipe nicely covers four servings of baked fish, baked potato, or steamed vegetables. Try it with an accompaniment of sweet & sour cabbage.

Tamari-ginger sauce

½ cup tamari

½ cup water

1 Tbs. dry sherry, or Chinese Rice Wine

1 Tbs. grated ginger

½ cup minced scallions

1 small clove crushed garlic

2 tsp. sesame oil

optional. (Add both or neither.)
{ 2 tsp. dark vinegar PLUS 2 tsp. sugar

whisk together. Let stand 15 minutes.

Serve this as a dipping sauce for Tempura Vegetables. It can be served at room temperature. It keeps very well, refrigerated, in a tightly closed container. This sauce can also be used for Chinese-style sautéed vegetables (see the instructions in the "Entrées" section). And, if you are a fish-lover, try marinated fish (include the vinegar and sugar) - Marinate raw fish several hours in Tamari-Ginger, then bake it until done.

Greek Lemon Sauce (w/ Egg)

~ for stuffed grape leaves
   plain or stuffed artichokes
   Greek pilaf or plain, cooked rice
   Baked Fish
                      ~ enough for 4 servings

3/4 cup boiling water

1½ tsp. cornstarch dissolved in 1½ tsp. water

1 egg (whole)

1 egg yolk

3 Tbs. fresh lemon juice

½ tsp. salt

① Stir cornstarch paste into boiling water. Boil for 1 minute.

② Beat egg plus yolk until light and fluffy. Add lemon juice, beating.

③ Gradually pour hot liquid into egg-lemon mixture, constantly beating
   (use a wire whisk.)

④ Return to pan. Heat gently, whisking, until slightly thickened. DON'T
   BOIL! Serve immediately.

Orange-Ginger Sauce

$\frac{1}{3}$ cup butter
$\frac{1}{3}$ cup flour (whole wheat and/or white)
$1\frac{1}{2}$ Tbs. freshly-grated ginger
1 large clove garlic
1 cup milk
1 cup orange juice
1 Tbs. tamari
1 tsp. grated orange rind
black pepper to taste

Melt the butter in a saucepan. Add the ginger and garlic and sauté a minute or two. Whisk in the flour; cook, whisking 3-4 minutes. Gradually add the milk, still whisking and cook (lowest heat) five minutes. Then add orange juice, tamari, pepper and orange rind and cook ten minutes longer, stirring occasionally.

Serve over baked fish filets or freshly-steamed or sautéed vegetables. This recipe serves 4-6.

Zippy Cheese Sauce

3 Tbs. flour

3 Tbs. butter

sautéed in 1 Tbs. butter with a dash of salt
{ ½ cup minced onion

1 clove crushed garlic

2 cups warmed milk

1 packed cup grated cheese
(your favorite)

1 Tbs. dry white wine

½ tsp. dry mustard

½ tsp. prepared horseradish

a few shakes tabasco sauce

Melt butter in saucepan. Whisk in flour (whole wheat pastry flour may be used. It'll give a heartier flavor.) and cook whisking for 2 minutes. Whisk in warmed milk; lower heat, and continue to stir frequently as it cooks until smooth and thick. (It's best to cook sauce either in a double boiler, or with a heat-absorbent pad under the pot.) Add remaining ingredients. Serve very hot. (Very good when served over steamed vegetables or omelettes.)

Impress your lunch guests with a

Broiled Openfaced
Sandwich

(1) On a slice of your favorite bread, spread a little butter,
   a layer of thinly-sliced apple
   a slice of your favorite cheese
   some cashews and/or walnuts

Broil under very low heat until nuts are lightly brown
and cheese bubbles.

"You can also hide some raisins under the cheese."
       —anonymous fan of hidden raisins.

(2) On rye or pumpernickel or herb bread:
   some fancy Dijon-type mustard
   some home-made mayonnaise
   a very thin slice of onion
   " " " " " tomato
   some thin rings of sweet red or green pepper
   a slice of the finest cheese in the room

Broil till cheese begins to turn brown.

Celebratory Sandwich Fillings

(1) Well, you can take some cream cheese (8oz.) and mash it with a ripe banana, a squirt of fresh lemon or lime, some raisins, and some chopped, toasted nuts. This will fill about four sandwiches. You can insert a slice of fresh pineapple. You can also opt to add some chopped dates, fresh pear or apple, or strawberries.

(2) If you are less inclined to decadence, try jazzing up your usual egg salad by ⓐ using Moosewood's Home-made Mayonnaise recipe, ⓑ adding some chopped, toasted almonds, along with fresh scallions and parsley, ⓒ a few dashes of paprika and dry mustard.

(3) On the other hand, if you are only moderately inclined to decadence, take the best peanut butter in the world (Your Favorite) and augment it with toasted sesame seeds and honey. Mix it all up. If you pack a lunch, try inserting some green seedless grapes into your sandwich. You will forget you put them there, and at lunchtime you'll get a pleasant surprise to cheer you up.

(4) Back to the cream cheese, try mashing it with your favorite herbs (dill? basil? oregano? tarragon? Discover.) and some chopped parsley, chives, tinily-diced cucumber, chopped watercress. Place very thin slices of water chestnut or radish on spread filling. Fresh spinach too, plus tomato, plus alfalfa sprouts.

(5) sesame-butter mashed with honey and lemon PLUS chopped dates ♡

(6) cashew butter.. with a few Fresh Peach Slices

(7) Mash 8 oz. softened cream cheese with ¾ cup finely-chopped, toasted walnuts and ½ cup chopped black olives. Spread on dark bread; serve open-faced, garnished with chopped scallions, strips of red pepper, thin slices of cucumber.

  For a special occasion, try all of the above for a fancy, assorted platter. Decorate with all kinds of cut raw vegetables and with orange slices, parsley sprigs, chunks of tomato.

Rarebit

... the old-fashioned Welsh cheese sauce, spiked with beer.

This sauce is definitely the backbone of a meal. It needs only a piece of toast underneath to make it complete, although the list of variations for serving is long.

For 6 servings:

3 Tbs. butter

3 Tbs. whole wheat flour

1½ cups beer or ale, room temperature

1 lb. cheddar cheese, coarsely-grated

optional:
1 clove garlic, crushed
(sauté in the butter)

1 tsp. dry mustard

½ tsp. prepared horseradish

a few drops of tabasco sauce

a few grindings of fresh, black pepper

In a medium-large saucepan, melt the butter. Whisk in the flour and dry mustard. Lower heat and cook, whisking, 5 minutes. Whisk in beer, and cook and whisk 8-10 more minutes, or until thick. Add remaining ingredients and cook over very low heat 8-10 minutes, stirring occasionally with a wooden spoon. Serve on toasted bread or English muffins, plain, or accompanied by apple or tomato slices, toasted walnuts, steamed broccoli or asparagus or sautéed mushrooms.

Grilled Vegetable Sandwiches

Each of these suggestions makes enough for four good-sized sandwiches. How much bread you'll need depends on whether you'll be broiling the sandwiches (open-faced) or grilling them in butter in a frying pan (closed – 2 pieces of bread). You can do any of these either way.

Have your filling ready ahead of time. Assemble the sandwiches right before serving. Garnish lavishly with fruit slices and vegetable sticks.

Broccoli & Friends

① 2 cups finely-chopped broccoli
½ cup finely-chopped onion
few dashes each: basil, thyme, black pepper
½ tsp. salt
2 Tbs. butter
¾ cup grated cheese (your favorite)

Sauté broccoli, onion and salt in butter until broccoli is bright green. Add herbs.
Spread onto toasted bread, top with cheese, and broil.
Serve immediately.

Eggplant

② 2½ cups minced eggplant
½ cup finely-chopped onion
2 Tbs. butter (or butter plus olive oil)
1 small clove crushed garlic
½ cup chopped black olives
juice from ½ lemon
salt and black pepper to taste
dash of cayenne
¾ cup grated cheddar

Sauté onion, garlic and eggplant, lightly salted, in butter and olive oil. When the eggplant is very soft, remove from heat. Add olives and seasonings.
Spread onto toast and broil or grill the cheese onto the filling.
Serve immediately.

Spicy Peppers
(a good use for day-old corn bread)

③ 2 large bell peppers, sliced
¾ cup chopped onion
½ tsp. ground cumin (or more)
1 Tbs. each: butter and olive oil
dash or two of cayenne
(optional: 1 small clove garlic)
salt and pepper to taste
1 cup grated mild, white cheese

Saute onions and garlic, lightly-salted, in olive oil and butter. When onion is translucent, add peppers and cumin. Remove from heat and season. Spread onto split, toasted corn bread, top with lots of cheese, and broil. Serve right away.

Bavarian Style

④ 1 cup, drained, sauerkraut
2 tomatoes, sliced
lots of dijon mustard
1 cup grated cheddar

This works best with rye or pumpernickel. Toast the bread. Spread it with mustard, sauerkraut and tomatoes. Top with cheese and broil or grill. Serve soon.

Zucchini-Parmesan Sandwich

⑤ 2 cups diced fresh zucchini
½ cup minced onion
1 clove crushed garlic
½ tsp. basil
½ tsp. oregano
2 Tbs. olive oil
salt, pepper
fresh tomato slices
½ cup freshly-grated parmesan

Sauté onion and garlic, with salt, basil and oregano, in olive oil until onion is translucent. Add zucchini and sauté until soft.
Spread onto toast, topped with thin slices of tomato and a sprinkling of fresh parmesan. This one should be broiled, not grilled. Parmesan loves to broil.

One hour to prepare,
including cornbread
and its baking.

Pepper & Onion Shortcake

6 servings

Make a batch of your favorite cornbread. (There are two recipes in the "Miscellaneous Baked Things" section of this book – or use your own personal, traditional recipe.) Prepare the following topping while the bread bakes, so it can be served as soon as the bread is done.

1 cup thinly-sliced onions

3 medium (fist-sized) sweet bell peppers, red and green, sliced into thin strips

3/4 cup sour cream

3/4 cup yogurt

1/4 cup butter

1/4-1/2 tsp. salt

paprika

black pepper

1/4 tsp. dill weed

Melt the butter in a heavy skillet or saucepan. Add the onions and salt. Turn the heat way down and cook very slowly until the onions are translucent (not brown). Add peppers, black pepper and dill. Cover and cook for 10 minutes. Add sour cream and yogurt. Keep warm over low heat until the cornbread is ready. Ladle the topping over split chunks of hot cornbread. (You might want to serve this in bowls.)

Pass around extra dill weed.

Sprinkle paprika onto each serving.

88

The Sandwich for Bleu Cheese Fans

~four servings~

This sandwich would win the approval of Henri Matisse, and of fans of Rainbows as well.

★ Okay, so, you take four modest slices of good rye or pumpernickel bread. Put them aside in a pile, and remember where you put them. We'll return to the Bread later.

★ Now, you take a couple of stalks of broccoli, and slice them into about 8-12 thin spears. Cut a medium bell pepper (red, if possible. But green will do.) into thin strips. Sauté these in a little butter until tender. Put these aside.

★ Thinly shred or grate one cup of each: raw cabbage, carrot and beet.

★ Thinly slice one small red onion. Keep all these cut and shredded raw vegetables in separate piles or containers.

★ Combine: 1 cup bleu cheese
            ½ cup yogurt
            ½ cup mayonnaise   purée together in the blender.
            1 Tbs. lemon juice   Add salt and pepper to taste.
            2 Tbs. vinegar

★ Cut 4 thin slices of mild, white cheese.

Now:

1- Toast the bread
2- Spread it with mustard.
3- Distribute the broccoli and peppers, laying them down flat.
4- Pile on layers of shredded raw vegetable (all except the onion)
5- Place a slice of cheese on top. Stick the sandwiches under the broiler until the cheese melts.
6- Ladle on lots of bleu cheese dressing.

Top with red onion slices. Serve at once.

Two Exotic Walnut Pâtés

Feta-Walnut Dip

yield: 2¾ cups

1 cup crumbled feta cheese

2 Tbs. olive oil

½ cup milk

1 cup chopped walnuts

dash of cayenne

1 tsp. paprika

> Spread this on crackers
> or pita bread
> or
> dip raw vegetables
> in it.

1- Soak the feta in water for an hour or two, to partially de-salt it.

2- Combine in the blender: 1 Tbs. olive oil, 3 Tbs. milk, ⅓ cup feta (drained) and ⅓ cup walnuts. Blend on low, then medium speed.

3- Gradually, while blender runs at medium speed, add remaining ingredients. Blend to a smooth paste. Chill.

Vegetable-Walnut Pâté

yield: 2 cups

-This one really does taste like chopped liver.

1½ cups cooked green beans, pulverized

2 hard-boiled eggs, grated

¼ cup toasted walnuts, pulverized   1-2 Tbs. mayonnaise

½ cup finely-minced onion, sautéed until soft in a little oil or butter

1-2 Tbs. dry, white wine   salt, black pepper, pinch of nutmeg

Combine everything and chill. Use as a sandwich spread or dip for raw vegetables and crackers.

Humus

about 6 servings

Begin soaking chickpeas early in the day.

You'll need cooking & cooling time as well.

Humus is a chickpea pâté of Middle-Eastern origins. It is a spicy and rich spread, full of protein. You can use it as a sandwich spread or an appetizer-dip (scoop it up with pieces of pocket bread and sticks of raw vegetables). You can also build an entire meal around a plateful of humus, vegetables and bread. It's filling enough.

1½ cups raw chickpeas, soaked 1½ hours and boiled until very soft (1½ hours)

3 medium cloves minced garlic

1½ tsp. salt

dash of tamari

juice from 2 medium lemons

3/4 cup tahini

¼ cup (packed) finely-minced parsley

lots of black pepper & dash of cayenne

¼ cup minced scallions

Mash chickpeas to a thick paste, using a food mill or grinder, or a masher.

Combine everything and chill thoroughly.

Taste to correct seasonings. Some people like extra garlic, tamari or tahini.

Eggplant Pâtés

Here are some variations on the theme of the Middle Eastern Eggplant. The eggplant pâté is not very widespread in this part of the world, and where heard of, it's usually thought of as an Incidental - an appetizer, side dish, or just plain Novelty to taste. (and exclaim that it tastes just like chopped liver.)

These recipes can be bases for meals, if you surround them with plenty of vegetables and bread to dip... beautiful, light summer dinners.

Baba Ganouj

This recipe makes enough to fill six people who are dipping vegetables and bread into it, and calling it Dinner.

Start this 3 hours ahead of time. Eggplants need slow baking and cooling.

2 medium-small eggplants

juice from one good-sized lemon

½ cup tahini

3 medium cloves garlic, crushed

½ cup finely-chopped parsley

1 tsp. salt (more, to taste)

¼ cup finely-minced scallions (optional)

lots of fresh black pepper

1 Tbs. olive oil

continued . . . .>

Baba Ganouj, continued

Preheat oven to 400°.

Cut off the stem-ends of the eggplants, and prick them* all over with a fork. Place them on an oven rack directly, and let them roast slowly until completely pooped (about 45 minutes.). When they are sagging, wrinkled, crumpled and totally soft, you'll know they're ready. Remove them gingerly from the oven, and wait until cool enough to handle. Scoop the insides out and mash well. Combine with all other ingredients, except olive oil. Chill the Ganouj completely, and drizzle the oil over the top just before serving.

* Eggplants, not stem-ends.

- -

Ganouj Variations

I. Follow the above instructions, adding

<u>1 cup finely-minced onions</u>
    and
<u>1 cup finely-minced mushrooms,</u>
which have been sauteed well together in olive oil, with a little extra salt.

II. Follow the above instructions, adding

1 cup yogurt or sour cream

½ tsp. ground cumin

few dashes of cayenne

mayonnaise to taste

- -

Spicy Eggplant Relish

Serve this as a condiment to almost anything- especially curries, humus, felafel, or Tabouli Salad. Or, use it as a dip or spread.

2 medium-small eggplants, cut into ½-inch cubes
3 Tbs. olive oil
1 cup chopped onion
1 cup chopped green pepper
1 tsp. cumin
salt and lots of cayenne
juice of one lemon

Cook onions and eggplant together in oil, with a little salt. Cook slowly, over low heat, until soft.

Add remaining ingredients, and season to taste. Serve hot or cold.

93

Guacamole

(Mexican Avocado Pâté)

Guacamole can be a salad topping, sandwich spread or dip. As a dip, it's best when scooped up with raw vegetables or tortilla chips (see below). This recipe serves 4-6.

Mix and chill.

This is the basic recipe. You can augment it with some or all of the options below.

{
2 ripe avocadoes, mashed
(medium-large)

juice of 1 lemon

2-3 cloves crushed garlic

½ tsp. salt (more, to taste)

chili powder and black pepper to taste
}

For Chunky Guacamole:

- minced green or red pepper
- 1 small, finely-minced red onion
- 1 small, chopped cucumber
- a chopped hard-cooked egg
- 1 medium, diced tomato
- ½ cup chopped olives

For Extra Creaminess:

Add, to taste:

Homemade mayonnaise (see salad chapter, "Special Salad Dressings")
or
sour cream
or
yogurt

. . . .

How to Make Your Own Tortilla Chips:

Take a dozen tortillas (raw ones), either home-made (recipe in "Miscellaneous Baked Things" chapter) or frozen, store-bought (defrost before unwrapping, or they'll dry out) and cut them into quarters (see Exhibit A).

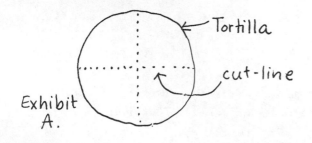

Tortilla

cut-line

Exhibit A.

Heat ½ inch of peanut, safflower or soy (or "vegetable") oil in a heavy skillet until it's hot enough to instantly sizzle a drop of water. Deep-fry the tortilla quarters until crisp and brown. Drain on a double thickness of paper towels.

94

Entrées

Vegetable Stroganoff

(sour cream-wine sauce
over vegetables
over noodles)

6 servings
1 hour to prepare

I. The Sauce

3 cups sour cream
1½ cups yogurt
3 Tbs. dry, red wine
1 cup chopped onion
½ pound chopped mushrooms
¾ tsp. salt
¼ tsp. dill weed
dash of tamari sauce
paprika
black pepper

2 Tbs. butter

Sauté onions and mushrooms in butter until onions
are soft. Combine all ingredients in the top of a double
boiler and heat gently about 30 minutes.

II. While the sauce simmers, steam 6 cups chopped, fresh
vegetables. Highly recommended:

Broccoli
Cauliflower   Carrots
Zucchini   Celery
                        Cabbage
Peppers   Cherry Tomatoes

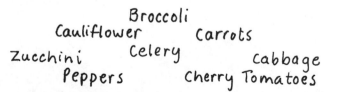

III. Cook 4 cups raw eggnoodles in boiling, salted water until
tender. Drain and butter.

Assemble the Stroganoff on a platter and garnish
with freshly-minced scallions.

Chilean Squash

1½ hours
to prepare

4-6 servings

4 cups cooked squash or pumpkin,
mashed or puréed

1 cup chopped onion

1½ cups chopped mixed red and green peppers

2-3 large cloves crushed garlic

1 tsp. ground cumin

4 beaten eggs

2 cups corn (fresh or frozen)

½ tsp. chili powder

1 cup grated cheddar

½ tsp. ground coriander

dash of cayenne (more to taste)

dash of black pepper

1 tsp. salt

2 Tbs. olive oil

① Saute onions, garlic and spices in olive oil until onions and
garlic are translucent. Add peppers and salt. Cover and cook
5-8 minutes.

② Add sauté to mashed squash, along with corn and beaten
eggs. Mix well. Taste to correct seasonings.

③ Spread into a buttered 2-quart casserole, and top with cheese.

350° oven   20 minutes, covered
               15 minutes, uncovered

Mushroom Curry

45 minutes to prepare

4-6 servings

4 Tbs. butter

2 cups chopped onion

2 cloves minced garlic

1 cup chopped celery

1½ lb. chopped mushrooms

(It's more interesting to combine spices than to use "curry powder")

{ 1 tsp. ground cumin

1 tsp. cinnamon

1 tsp. turmeric

1 tsp. powdered ginger

½ tsp. dry mustard }

½ tsp. ground cloves

3 Tbs. shredded, unsweetened coconut

1 Tbs. honey

juice from 1 lemon

3 large tomatoes

2 large cooking apples

1½ tsp. salt (or more, to taste)

lots of ground black pepper

water to steam (about ¾ cup)

delicious topping { 1 cup sliced almonds sautéed in 2 Tbs. sweet butter

In a large skillet begin cooking onions and garlic in butter. After a few minutes add salt and spices. When onions are soft, add celery and mushrooms. You may want to add about ½ cup water at this point, to help prevent sticking (and to make a nice broth.) Mix well, cover, and simmer about 5-8 minutes (low heat.)

When celery is slightly tender, add apples and tomatoes (both in 1½" slices) and coconut. Mix and continue cooking until everything is just tender, not too mushy. (Additional water might be needed.) Turn off heat. Add honey and lemon juice; mix and let sit, covered.

Serve curry after it has sat for a few minutes. It tastes best when served over rice, with sautéed almonds on top.

Carrot-Mushroom Loaf

1 cup chopped onion
4½ cups grated carrots
1 lb. chopped mushrooms
5 eggs
2 cloves garlic
1 cup fresh, whole wheat breadcrumbs
1 cup grated cheddar cheese
¼ cup butter
salt
pepper
basil
thyme

Crush garlic into melting butter. Add onions and mushrooms and sauté till soft.

Combine all ingredients (saving half the breadcrumbs and cheese for the top). Season to taste.

Spread into buttered oblong baking pan. Sprinkle with remaining breadcrumbs and cheese. Dot with butter.

Bake 350° 30 minutes covered
5 uncovered
(or until browned.)

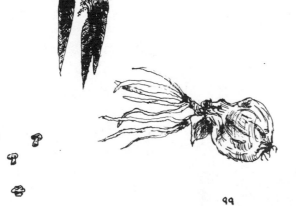

Soy Gevult:

soybeans and vegetables
in sour cream-black mushroom sauce

6-8 wholesome, exotic
servings

[→ Begin soaking beans
5 hours in advance]

[1½-2 hours to
prepare (after
beans are cooked),
including baking.]

Part I.

Cover with water in
saucepan. Cook 1¾
hours, or until tender.
When still hot (and
drained), toss with ....

{ 2 cups uncooked soybeans (soaked 3 hours)
2 tsp. salt

1 cup sour cream

1½ oz. dried black mushrooms
2½ cups boiling water

Part II.

Place mushrooms in bowl. Pour
in the water. Cover; let stand
20 minutes. Drain mushrooms
thoroughly, squeezing out excess
water. SAVE ALL THE WATER!
It holds flavor secrets. Slice
the mushrooms thinly.

Part III.

Melt the butter in a
saucepan. Add onion,
garlic, sliced black
mushrooms from Part II,
and salt. After 5 min-
utes, stir in flour.
Keep stirring + cooking
5 more minutes.

{ 1½ cups chopped onion
2 cloves crushed garlic
3 Tbs. butter
3 Tbs. flour
1 tsp. salt
2 Tbs. tamari
2 Tbs. sherry

Add black mushroom water, sherry, and tamari. Cook, stirring frequently, over
very low heat 8-10 minutes, or until thickened and smooth.

Part IV.

Steam up some of your favorite vegetables. Carrot, cabbage,
zucchini .... whatever. Recommended amount: about 6 cups' worth,
steamed. (1 small head cabbage, one medium sliced carrot, one smallish
zucchini, for example.)

Part V.

Combine everything in large casserole. Add
2 more Tbs. sherry
2 more Tbs. tamari
lots of black pepper.

Bake, covered, 45-50
minutes at 350°.

Whole Wheat Macaroni~Russian Style

6-8 servings $1\frac{1}{2}$ hours to prepare (including baking)

COMBINE:

    $1\frac{1}{2}$ cups sour cream
    2 cups cottage cheese
    1 cup grated cheddar
    1 red onion, thinly sliced
    2 chopped scallions
    1 chopped green pepper

SAUTÉ IN BUTTER:

    2 cups shredded cabbage
    $\frac{1}{2}$# sliced mushrooms
    1 chopped carrot
    1 tsp. carraway seeds

BOIL IN SALTED WATER
TILL JUST UNDERDONE:

    2 cups raw whole wheat
        macaroni
          ~ drain and butter

Combine everything. Add 2 Tbs. tamari sauce and lots of fresh black pepper.

Bake in a buttered casserole, covered, at 350°
40 minutes.

OPTIONAL ADDITIONS:

    toasted cashews
    "   sunflower or sesame
               seeds
    chopped fresh spinach

serve with fresh tomato slices (sprinkle them with basil)

Greek Pilaf

The Greek Pilaf is a basic way of preparing rice as a filling for grape leaves, artichokes or Greek-style eggplant. (p.115). It is delicious enough to serve by itself also, or as an accompaniment to sautéed vegetables or baked fish.

1 cup minced onion ⎫
2 cloves crushed garlic ⎪ sauté until
1 stalk minced celery ⎬ onions are
¼ cup sunflower seeds ⎪ soft. Then mix with
2-3 Tbs. olive oil ⎭

⎧ 2½ cups cooked (1¼ cups
⎪ raw) brown rice
⎪ 1-2 tsp. dried mint
⎨ juice from 1 lemon
⎪ ¼ cup freshly-chopped
⎪ parsley
⎩ salt and pepper to taste

Serve topped with crumbled feta cheese, or Lemon-egg sauce. (p.80).

This Pilaf will make about 6 8-leaf servings of:

Stuffed Grape Leaves

to Stuff an Artichoke

These can be a main dish or an appetizer, depending on the size of the leaves. If you have grapevines in your yard, the best time of year to pick leaves for stuffing is early June. Earlier, they'll be too small; later, too tough. Use the leaves fresh, or preserve them in salt water in tightly-closed jars. Or, you can buy preserved leaves in the Imported Food section of most grocery stores.

To Fill:

Place a leaf down flat, stem-end toward you. Place a heaping Tbs. (more or less) of filling near the base, and roll tightly, folding in the sides. Bake 20-25 minutes on an oiled tray, covered, at 350°. Top with Lemon-egg sauce (p.80).

The above pilaf will stuff about 6 medium artichokes.

Cook the artichokes, as you normally would, in lots of boiling water until tender enough to pull the leaves out easily. Drain and cool until it's not too hot to handle them.

Grab hold of the very tip-most leaf-cluster and yank it out.  Stick a teaspoon into the cavity and scoop out the choke (hairy stuff), being careful not to scoop out the heart (tender, smooth stuff below choke.) Spread outer leaves and fill with pilaf. Bake, covered, at 350° until heated through (20 minutes).

BULGARIAN PEPPER AND CHEESE DELIGHT

I. 4 cups minced green peppers

1½ cups sliced mushrooms

1½ cups chopped onions

2-3 Tbs. butter

1½ hours to prepare, including baking

6-8 servings

II.

1½ Tbs. tamari

1½ Tbs. sherry

1 tsp. marjoram

½-1 tsp. salt (to taste)

black pepper to taste

III.

1½ cups raw bulghar soaked in } *
1½ cups boiling water

1½ cups cottage cheese

¾ cup feta cheese

4 beaten, lightly-salted eggs

paprika

Sauté onions in butter until translucent. Add peppers and mushrooms. Continue to cook until peppers are just becoming tender. Remove from heat.

Add all of Group II to sautéed vegetables and mix well.

Crumble the feta cheese and combine with the cottage cheese.

Butter a 2-quart casserole or a 9"x13" baking pan. Spread in bulghar, and cover it with a layer of vegetables. Add the mixed cheeses, and spread them around as evenly as possible. Pour the beaten eggs over everything and dust with paprika.

350° oven ~ Bake 40-45 minutes, uncovered. Let stand for 10 minutes before serving.

* Soak the bulghar for at least 15 minutes. It will still be crunchy, but this will allow it to absorb liquid from the other ingredients.

```
┌ ∙∙∙∙∙∙∙∙∙∙∙∙∙∙∙∙∙∙∙∙∙∙∙∙∙∙∙∙∙∙∙∙∙∙ ┐
∙        ★ GADO-GADO ★           ∙
∙      ~ an Indonesian dish       ∙
∙      with spicy peanut sauce~   ∙
└ ∙∙∙∙∙∙∙∙∙∙∙∙∙∙∙∙∙∙∙∙∙∙∙∙∙∙∙∙∙∙∙∙∙∙ ┘
```

approximately   6-8 servings
one hour
to prepare

★ The Sauce:

1 cup chopped onion
2 medium cloves crushed garlic
1 cup good, pure peanut butter
1 Tbs. honey
¼ tsp. cayenne pepper (more, to taste)
juice of 1 lemon
1-2 tsp. freshly-grated ginger root
1 bay leaf
1 Tbs. cider vinegar
3 cups water
½-1 tsp. salt
dash of tamari
2 Tbs. butter for frying

In a saucepan, cook the onions, garlic, bay leaf and ginger in butter, lightly salted. When onion becomes translucent add remaining ingredients. Mix thoroughly. Simmer on lowest possible heat 30 minutes, stirring occasionally.

★ Underneath the Sauce:

The sauce goes over an artful arrangement of combined cooked and raw vegetables. Extra protein comes from garnishes of tofu chunks (bean curd) and hard-cooked egg slices. Base your arrangement on a bed of fresh spinach. Here are some recommended vegetables and garnishes:

Garnish with:

a drizzle of sesame oil
apples
lemons
oranges
raisins
toasted seeds & nuts

shredded cabbage ⎫
carrot slices   ⎬ steamed or raw
celery slices   ⎭

broccoli spears   ⎫
fresh, whole green beans ⎬ steamed

fresh, raw mung bean sprouts
tofu chunks, either raw, or
        sautéed in oil with sesame seeds
pieces of egg

40 minutes to prepare;
40 minutes to bake.

3 medium eggplants

1½ cup finely-chopped onion

1¼ tsp. minced garlic

2 lbs. ricotta cheese

1 heaping, packed cup grated
    mozzarella

2 large, sliced tomatoes

¾ cup wheat germ, mixed with
1 tsp. each ~ oregano & basil

salt and pepper

6-8 servings
Preheat oven to 375°F.

   Slice the eggplants into ⊙s. Salt lightly. Bake 15 minutes (or until tender) on an oiled tray. When eggplant is done sprinkle it with the wheat germ mixture. Turn oven down to 350°.

   Sauté the onions and garlic in butter until soft. Combine with the cheeses. Oil an oblong pan. Arrange a sandwich of eggplant-cheese-tomato-eggplant-tomato. Cover for the first 35 baking minutes. Uncover for the last five.

Lentil-Walnut Burgers

4-6 servings, depending upon size of patties and hunger of participants.

NOTE: uncooked burgers may be individually wrapped and frozen.

PART 1:

3/4 cup dry lentils
1½ cups water
2 tsp. cider vinegar

Bring lentils and water to a boil in a saucepan. Lower the heat, and simmer, partly-covered 30 minutes, or until lentils are soft, and liquid is gone. Place in large-ish bowl. Add vinegar, and mash.

PART 2:

1 Tbs. butter
1 cup finely-minced onion
1-2 cloves garlic, crushed
10 large mushrooms, minced
½ cup finely-minced walnuts
1 small stalk minced celery
1 tsp. salt
lots of fresh black pepper
½ tsp. dry mustard
1 Tbs. dry sherry

Sauté all of these together over medium-low heat 10-15 minutes, or until all is tender.

Add to the mashed lentils, and mix well.

½ cup raw wheat germ — Mix this in, too.

- Chill for about 1 hour before forming patties.
- Form 4-inch burgers, and fry in butter until brown,
OR- broil about 8 minutes on each side.

OPTIONAL: ~ melt some cheese on top.
~ sprinkle with dried basil.

Broccoli Mushroom Noodle Casserole

1¼ hours to prepare, including baking

6 servings: quite filling

chop & saute in butter until tender
{
2 stalks fresh broccoli (use stems as well as flowers - shave their tough outer skin and slice thinly.)

1 lb. fresh mushrooms

1 large onion
}

Salt and pepper lightly. Remove from heat and toss with ¼ cup dry white wine.

Beat 3 eggs in a large bowl. Whisk in 3 cups ricotta or cottage cheese (or a combination), and 1 cup sour cream.

Boil 3 cups raw wide, flat egg noodles in salted water until slightly underdone. Drain and butter.

Remove sautéed vegetables from pan to cheese mixture with slotted spoon. Add noodles and either 2 Tbs. wheat germ or ¼ cup fine bread crumbs.

Spread into buttered 9x13" baking pan. Top with more wheat germ or breadcrumbs and 1 cup grated sharp cheddar cheese.

Bake
--→ covered for 30 minutes
--→ uncovered for 15 minutes more

350° oven

Vericheesey Casserole

8 servings

Note: This recipe calls for 2 cups cooked soybeans and 2 cups cooked brown rice. Begin soaking <u>1 cup raw soybeans</u> 3½-4 hours before assembling the casserole. Cover them with water and soak 2 hours. Place soaked beans in a saucepan with ½ tsp. salt and lots of water. Cook 1½ hours, or until tender. Drain well. Use <u>1 cup raw brown rice.</u> Simmer the rice in 1⅔ cups boiling water, covered, for 20-25 minutes.

2 cups cooked soybeans
2 cups cooked brown rice
4 lightly-beaten eggs
2 cups (1lb.) cottage or ricotta cheese,
     or a combination

1 cup grated mozzarella
½ lb. chopped mushrooms
1 cup chopped onion
2-3 cloves crushed garlic
1 tsp. each: basil, thyme, marjoram
2 Tbs. tamari
salt, black pepper, and cayenne to taste
4 Tbs. butter
½ cup grated parmesan ⎫
½ cup fine bread crumbs ⎬ combined
2 medium tomatoes, thinly sliced.

1) Sauté onions, garlic, mushrooms and herbs in butter, until onions are soft.

2) Combine all but the last three ingredients.

3) Spread mixture into a large, buttered oblong pan.

4) Top with sliced tomatoes and combined parmesan and crumbs.

Bake in a 350° oven, uncovered, 40 minutes.

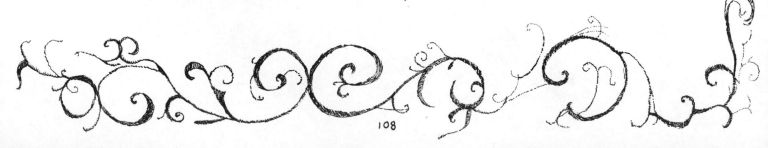

Stuffed Cabbage

1½ hours
to prepare

6 servings
2 rolls each

1 large head green cabbage

1 medium carrot, diced

1 cup chopped onion

3 Tbs. butter

1 small clove crushed garlic

¼ cup sunflower seeds

¾ cup raw cashew pieces

salt
pepper
} to taste

1 stalk chopped celery

2 cups ricotta cheese

¼ cup raisins or currants

1 cup chopped apple

juice from 1 lemon

1-2 Tbs. tamari

1 Tbs. honey

extra butter

① Parboil the cabbage in a kettle of water 10-15 minutes, or until outer leaves are easily removeable. Remove the 1st 12 leaves. Make sure the cabbage is cooked well enough so leaves will not break when rolled, but not so well that they disintegrate. If you can't get enough large-enough-to-stuff leaves from one cabbage, parboil two. Save cabbage insides to use for another dish.

② Sauté vegetables (not apple), nuts and seeds in butter until onion is transparent and nuts roasted. Combine the sauté (drain it well!) with remaining ingredients and season to taste.

③ Place 3-4 Tbs. filling near the base of each cabbage leaf. Roll tightly, folding in sides. Place on buttered sheet and brush with extra butter. Cover and bake until heated through (about 25 minutes at 325°).

Serve topped with yogurt or sour cream,
on a bed of rice.

Vegetarian Chili

6-8 servings

Start beans 4-5 hours early. Several hours to prepare + cook.

2½ cups raw kidney beans

1 cup raw bulghar

1 cup tomato juice

4 cloves crushed garlic

1½ cups chopped onion

1 cup each, chopped:
- celery
- carrots
- green peppers

2 cups chopped, fresh tomatoes

juice of ½ lemon

1 tsp. ground cumin

1 tsp. basil

1 tsp. chili powder (more, to taste)

salt and pepper

3 Tbs. tomato paste

3 Tbs. dry red wine

dash of cayenne (more, to taste)

olive oil for sauté (about 3 Tbs.)

① Put kidney beans in a saucepan and cover them with 6 cups of water. Soak 3-4 hours. Add extra water and 1 tsp. salt. Cook until tender (about 1 hour.) Watch the water level, and add more, if necessary.

② Heat tomato juice to a boil. Pour over raw bulghar. Cover and let stand at least 15 minutes. (It will be crunchy, so it can absorb more later.)

③ Sauté onions and garlic in olive oil. Add carrots, celery and spices. When vegetables are almost done, add peppers. Cook until tender.

④ Combine all ingredients and heat together gently — either in kettle over double boiler, or covered, in a moderate oven.

Serve topped with cheese & parsley.

Swiss Cheese and Mushroom Quiche

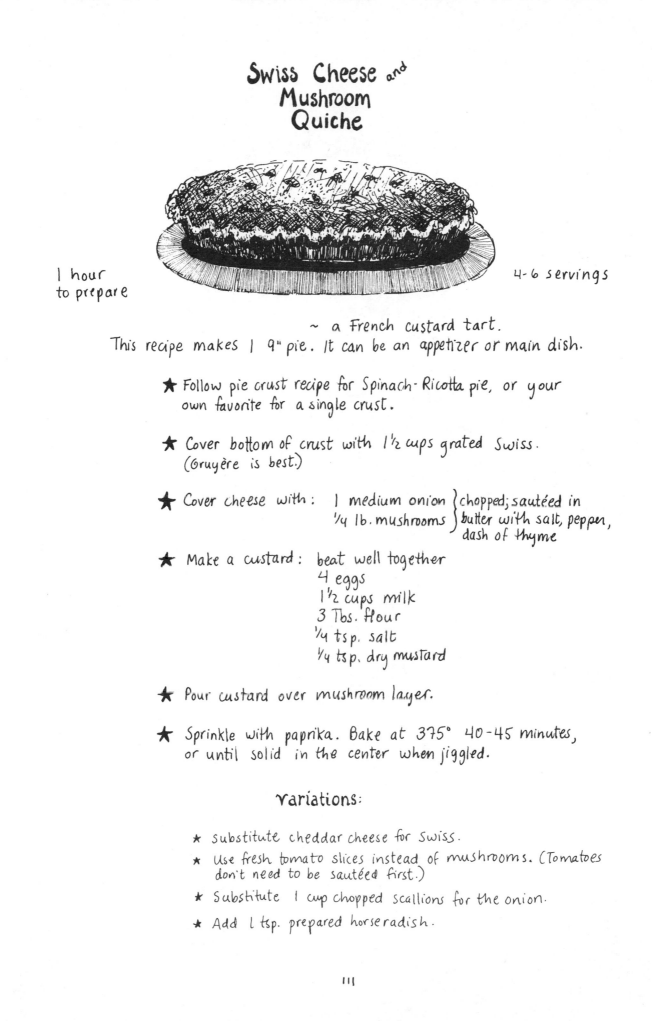

1 hour to prepare

4-6 servings

~ a French custard tart.
This recipe makes 1 9" pie. It can be an appetizer or main dish.

★ Follow pie crust recipe for Spinach-Ricotta pie, or your own favorite for a single crust.

★ Cover bottom of crust with 1½ cups grated Swiss. (Gruyère is best.)

★ Cover cheese with: 1 medium onion } chopped; sautéed in
1/4 lb. mushrooms } butter with salt, pepper, dash of thyme

★ Make a custard: beat well together
4 eggs
1½ cups milk
3 Tbs. flour
1/4 tsp. salt
1/4 tsp. dry mustard

★ Pour custard over mushroom layer.

★ Sprinkle with paprika. Bake at 375° 40-45 minutes, or until solid in the center when jiggled.

variations:

★ substitute cheddar cheese for Swiss.
★ Use fresh tomato slices instead of mushrooms. (Tomatoes don't need to be sautéed first.)
★ Substitute 1 cup chopped scallions for the onion.
★ Add 1 tsp. prepared horseradish.

noodle kugel

1¼ hours to prepare,
including baking

6-8 servings

3 eggs
1½ cups cottage cheese
3/4 cup sour cream (or yogurt)
8 oz. cream cheese
½ tsp. vanilla extract
2 tsp. cinnamon
¼ cup honey
few dashes salt

} Beat together until smooth.

2 medium cooking apples
OR
2 fresh, ripe peaches

}, sliced.

4 cups (raw) wide, flat egg noodles, boiled in salted water until just barely tender. Drain and butter.

COMBINE EVERYTHING.

Spread into well-buttered casserole.

Top with a mixture of {
1 cup bread crumbs
2 tsp. cinnamon
¼ cup wheat germ
¼ cup brown sugar

Dot with butter.

Bake uncovered, 35 minutes at 375°.

the pancake:

> 1 cup flour
> 1 cup milk
> 1 egg
> 1 Tbs. oil
> $\frac{1}{4}$ tsp. salt

beat in blender until smooth

Heat a few drops of oil in a 6" crêpe or omelette pan. When pan is hot, pour in enough batter to coat bottom of pan and slightly ('/8") up the sides. Pour excess batter off.(back into batter.) When pancake appears to solidify (this should be over moderate heat) lift the edges gently and flip it over with a small spatula. Turn out onto clean, dry towel or wooden surface.

This recipe should make 6-8 crêpes. You may want to double or triple it, as some batter may be lost to early mistakes. Also, crêpes are very light and delightful, and depending on what you fill them with, a person could consume quite a few.

What to put in your crêpes?

(1) Sliced Apples, sautéed in butter until tender, with lemon juice, honey and cinnamon. Try grating in some cheddar cheese. Top the crêpes with yogurt and toasted walnuts or almonds.

(2) Cheese-Herb Filling: 1½ cups cottage or ricotta cheese
        a minced scallion / dash of basil / fresh-chopped parsley

Mix cheese and herbs. Season with salt and pepper. Fill each crêpe with 3-4 Tbs. filling. Grill lightly in butter. Serve topped with sour cream or spinach-yogurt sauce. Garnish with tomato slices.

(3) Fresh Steamed or Sautéed Vegetables: Spinach and Mushrooms, sautéed in butter; Broccoli or Asparagus Spears; Whole Green beans. Heat the crêpes gently on a buttered tray. Serve topped with one of the many sauces in the "sauce" chapter. (Experiment on yourself.)

(4) White Rabbit Salad is great filling for brunch crêpes. (see p.45)

(5) Ratatouille is good filling for dinner crêpes. Cool the Ratatouille first, mix it with grated cheese, fill and heat the crêpes." p.119)

2 TIPS: - Make the pancakes & filling in advance, but assemble just before heating or serving. Otherwise they'll get soggy.
- Crêpes can be served hot, cold or room-temperature.

STUFFED EGGPLANT I.
"HIPPIE-STYLE"

6 servings

3 medium eggplants
½ lb. chopped mushrooms
2 cloves minced garlic
1 cup chopped onion
1½ cups cottage cheese
1 cup cooked brown rice*
1 cup grated cheddar
salt and pepper to taste
½ tsp. thyme
a few drops of tabasco
¼ cup toasted sunflower seeds
¼ cup freshly-chopped parsley
butter for sauté (about 3 Tbs)
paprika

• Slice the eggplants in half lengthwise. Use soup spoons and/or grapefruit spoons to scoop out the insides, right down to ¼" of skin.

• Chop the eggplant innards into ½" bits, and sauté it with the onions, garlic, mushrooms, salt and pepper until onions are clear and eggplant soft.

Combine everything, and season it according to your nature. Stuff the shells generously and with love. Dust with paprika, and bake uncovered** on buttered tray.
      350° oven   35-40 minutes

(* ½ cup raw)

** Cover, if it seems dry

STUFFED EGGPLANT II.
"MIMI'S ELEGANT"

6 servings

3 medium eggplants
2 cloves crushed garlic
1 bay leaf
1 cup chopped onion
2 medium green peppers
2 medium (3 small) tomatoes
1 heaping tsp. basil
¼ tsp. tarragon } more, to taste
¼ tsp. oregano }
2 cups ricotta cheese
½ cup grated parmesan
1 cup fine bread crumbs
salt and pepper to taste
olive oil for sauté (3 Tbs.)

• Slice eggplants in half lengthwise, and bake them face-down on an oiled tray at 350° for 20-25 minutes. Scoop out the insides and mince them.

• Sauté eggplant insides with the onions, garlic, bay leaf and peppers until onions are clear. Combine with everything except half the parmesan and the bread crumbs. Let stand 20 minutes, then drain off all excess liquid.

• Stuff the shells. Top with combined bread crumbs and remaining parmesan.
      350° oven   35-40 minutes, uncovered.

STUFFED EGGPLANT III.
"Greek Style"

6 servings

3 medium Eggplants   Greek Pilaf (p.102)   1 cup crumbled feta cheese

Slice eggplants in half lengthwise, and bake face-down on an oiled tray at 350° for 20-25 minutes. Scoop out insides and mince.

• Follow recipe for Greek Pilaf — make it 1½ times. Combine eggplant, pilaf and feta. Stuff the shells and bake for 25-30 minutes at 350°.

Mushroom Moussaka

a Greek Eggplant Casserole
with two rich sauces

2 hours to prepare,
including baking

·1· Slice **3** medium eggplants ½" thick. Salt lightly and bake on an oiled cooky sheet   350°   15 minutes or until tender.

·2· MUSHROOM SAUCE: Slice 2 lbs. mushrooms. Sauté in butter with 1 large, chopped onion and 2 cloves minced garlic – in saucepan.

add~   6 oz. tomato paste
¼ cup freshly-chopped parsley
dash each- oregano and basil
½ tsp. salt
fresh pepper
dash cinnamon
¼ cup dry red wine

~simmer until liquid is absorbed

add last - ½ cup bread crumbs
½ cup grated parmesan or cheddar
4 beaten eggs.

~remove from heat

·3· WHITE SAUCE: ½ cup butter ~ melt over low flame
½ cup flour ~ whisk into butter (keep motion constant.)
Resulting paste is called a <u>roux</u>. (pronounce "roo")
(as in kanga-___)
2½ cups warm milk - whisk in.

COOK, WHISKING UNTIL THICK. BEAT IN:

4 egg yolks

·4· Butter a large casserole. Cover the bottom with eggplant slices, then half the mushroom sauce. Add remaining eggplant and cover with remaining mushroom sauce. Top with white sauce. Sprinkle on bread crumbs and extra grated cheese.

350° oven- bake 35 minutes, covered
15 minutes, uncovered

Cauliflower Marranca

If grain is pre·cooked:
1 hour to prepare,
including baking

5-6 servings

1 lb mushrooms, sliced .... sauté in butter
1 large onion, chopped   with juice of 1 lemon

1 large head cauliflower, ... sauté with 3 cloves
        in flower pieces   crushed garlic, basil,
                                    salt and pepper

3 cups cooked brown rice or millet ... salted,
                                        buttered.

2½ cups grated cheese of your choice

            Combine Everything.

        Bake, covered, ½ hour at 350°.

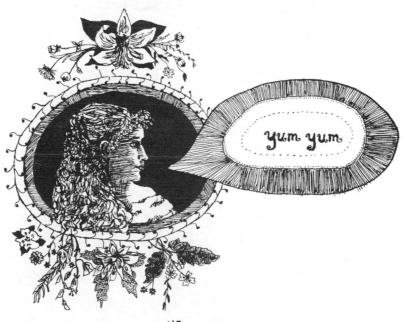

117

Polenta and Spicy Vegetables

I. POLENTA · SIX SERVINGS . . . . 15 minutes to prepare

Polenta is a cheesey corn meal mush which originated in Italy. It's simple and quick, and very filling and delicious. Serve it under sautéed fresh vegetables, Ratatouille (opposite) or spicy Spanish-style vegetables (below). Always serve polenta very hot, and top the vegetables with ricotta or grated sharp cheese. (Hint: prepare vegies first, so polenta doesn't sit too long.)

1½ cups corn meal (yellow)
1 cup cold water
1 tsp. salt
3½-4 cups boiling water
1 packed cup grated cheddar
grated parmesan to taste

Combine corn meal, cold water and salt. Mash into a uniform paste. Add to rapidly boiling water, lower the heat and beat with a wire whisk while it cooks. Cook for 10-12 minutes. It should be the consistency of thick breakfast cereal. Mix in the cheese. Keep warm in double boiler until serving time. (Best to serve as soon as possible.)

II. SPICY VEGIES

Follow the recipe for Ratatouille on the following page, with these changes:

① <u>omit</u> bay leaf, basil, marjoram, rosemary and oregano

② <u>Add</u> 1 tsp. each cumin, ground coriander and chili powder, plus hot sauce or cayenne to taste.

③ Optional: add ½ cup chopped spanish olives.

Ratatouille

Mediterranean vegetable stew

4-6 servings

1 medium onion (fist-size), chopped
2 medium bell peppers, in strips or cubes
2 small, or 1 medium, zucchini, cubed
          (or summer squash, or a combination)
1 small eggplant, cubed
4 cloves crushed garlic
2 medium tomatoes, in chunks
1 bay leaf
1 tsp. each: basil, marjorm
½ tsp. oregano
dash of ground rosemary
3 Tbs. burgundy (or dry, red wine of your choice)
½ cup tomato juice
2 Tbs. tomato paste
2 tsp. salt (approximately)
black pepper to taste
¼ cup olive oil
freshly-chopped parsley

    Heat olive oil in large, heavy cooking pot. Crush the garlic into the oil. Add bay leaf and onion; salt lightly. Sauté over medium heat until onion begins to turn transparent. Add eggplant, wine and tomato juice. Add herbs. Stir to mix well, then cover and simmer 10-15 minutes over low heat. When eggplant is tender enough to be easily pricked by a fork, add zucchini and peppers. Cover and simmer 10 minutes. Add salt and pepper, tomatoes and tomato paste. Mix well. Continue to stew until all vegetables are tender. (How tender is Tender? Do a taste test and decide what seems right to you.)

    Just before serving, mix in the fresh parsley.

    Serve on a bed of rice, or in a bowl, accompanied by some good french bread. Top with grated cheese and chopped black olives.

ZUCCANOES

(or, Stuffed Zucchini)

If you don't have any pre-cooked soybeans or brown rice hanging around in your refrigerator, put up ½ cup raw rice to cook before you begin.

Preparation time: 1¼ hours,
including baking.

to serve 6:

Slice 3 medium zucchini (or summer squash) in half lengthwise. Scoop out insides, leaving ¼" rim so canoe stays intact.

Sauté in
butter: chopped zucchini innards
½ lb. chopped mushrooms
a large, chopped onion
1 clove crushed garlic
2 Tbs. sunflower seeds

season with Rosemary
Basil
& Thyme

Beat 3 eggs. Mix with 1½ cups cottage cheese, ¼ cup wheat germ, 3 Tbs. tamari sauce, dash Worcestershire sauce, a couple shakes Tabasco sauce, 1 cup grated cheddar, 1 cup cooked soybeans and/or brown rice. Add the sautéed vegetables.

Stuff the canoes generously. Sprinkle with Paprika.

Bake 40 minutes at 350°.

Serve topped with extra grated cheese or sour cream.

Spinach-Rice Casserole

1¼ hours to prepare, including baking.   4-6 servings

Put this up to cook before you begin. { 4 cups cooked brown rice (scant 2 cups raw, cooked in 3 cups water)

2 lbs. raw, chopped spinach
1 cup chopped onion
2 cloves minced garlic
3 Tbs. butter
4 beaten eggs
1 cup milk
1½ cups grated cheddar
¼ cup chopped parsley
2 Tbs. tamari
½ tsp. salt (more, to taste)
a few dashes each - nutmeg, cayenne
¼ cup sunflower seeds
paprika

Sauté onions and garlic with salt in butter. When onions are soft, add spinach. Cook 2 minutes.

Combine with all ingredients except sunflower seeds and paprika. Spread into buttered casserole and sprinkle   "   "   "   " on top.

Bake, covered, 35 minutes at 350°.

Mushroom Strudel

1½-2 hours to prepare,
including baking

10 filo (strudel) leaves
½ lb. butter

filling
{
1 lb. chopped mushrooms (4 cups packed, raw)
1 tsp. salt
freshly-grated black pepper
½ tsp. ground caraway or dill seed
8 oz. cream cheese (you can substitute ½
                                pot or cottage cheese)
½ cup sour cream
½ cup yogurt
1 cup fine bread crumbs
¼ cup freshly-chopped parsley
2 scallions, minced (include as much of the greens
                                as possible.)
juice from 1 lemon
}

2 Tbs. poppyseeds ...

...a well-buttered baking tray

FILLING: Steam the mushrooms and drain them, squeezing out as much excess liquid as possible. (Save the liquid for soup stock.) Cut the cream cheese into the hot mushrooms, tossing until the cheese melts. Add remaining filling ingredients. Mix well.

TO ASSEMBLE: Melt the butter. Lay a leaf of filo flat on a wooden surface (or a formica counter) and brush with melted butter. Add another leaf and brush with more butter. (Be generous with the butter.) Continue to stack the leaves until you have a pile of 5 (five.). Apply half the filling across the width of the leaves, over a 3-4" space: and roll it up tightly. Brush the top with butter and sprinkle on 1 Tbs. poppyseeds. Using a spatula, transfer to buttered tray. Repeat this ritual to make a second roll.   Slash each roll into 3rds on the diagonal. Bake 25 minutes at 375°. Serve hot.

← filling

roll up in this direction

✶ ✶ ✶ ✶ ✶ ✶ ✶ ✶ ✶ ✶ Spinach-Ricotta Pie ✶

~1 9" pie~

3 hours to prepare, assemble, and bake.

The Crust

Try to work quickly so ingredients stay cold.

Cut together 1 cup flour (4/5 white plus 1/5 whole wheat is nice) (that's approximate, of course) and 1/3 cup cold butter. Use a pastry cutter or two forks, or a food processor fitted with a steel blade.

When the mixture is uniformly blended, add about 3 Tbs. cold buttermilk (or water. But buttermilk really. Specialness is worth it.) ~or enough so that mixture holds together enough to form a ball.

Chill the dough at least one hour.

★ ★ ★ ★ ★ ★ ★ ★ ★ ★ ★

The Filling

1 lb. ricotta cheese
3 beaten eggs
1/2 lb. chopped spinach ⎱ sautéed in butter with black pepper, 1/2 tsp.
1 small, diced onion ⎰ salt, 1/2 tsp. basil
3 Tbs. flour
1/2 cup grated sharp cheese
dash nutmeg

Mix everything together, blending well. Spread into unbaked pie shell. Top with 1 cup sour cream spread to edges of crust and a generous application of paprika.

375° oven   40-45 minutes

Serve piping ♫ hot.

Lasagne

Have ready:

6-8 servings
1½ hours

1) Tomato sauce (page 66.)

2) 12 lasagne noodles, ½-cooked, drained, rinsed in cold water

3) Filling: 2 cups ricotta/cottage cheese plus 2 beaten eggs, salt & pepper. (optional: ½ lb. raw spinach, chopped, plus dash of nutmeg, plus 2 Tbs. wheat germ)

4)   1 lb. shredded mozzarella cheese

5) ½ cup grated parmesan or romano cheese

6) A 9x13" pan.

Proceedings:

1) Spread a little sauce over bottom of pan
2) Cover with a layer of noodles (⅓ the noodles)
3) Put a blotch of filling here and there. Use ½ the filling.
4) Sauce (⅓ the remaining sauce)
5) ½ the mozzarella hither and thither.
6) Another ⅓ the noodles
7) Remaining filling, followed by
8) Sauce (another ⅓), which gets covered by
9) Remaining mozzarella.
10) Every last noodle
11) Ultimate dosage of sauce
12) The parmesan or romano.

Bake 45 minutes
375°.

Let stand 10 minutes before serving.

124

zucchini parmesan

eggplant parmesan

eggplant lasagne

zucchini lasagne

6-8 servings
1½ hours

① Make a batch of Italian Tomato Sauce (p. 66).

② Prepare your eggplant and/or zucchini as indicated below.

③ Prepare your cheeses and assemble your concoction.

To Prepare the Vegetables:

Use 4 medium zucchini or 2 large-ish eggplants. Slice zucchini 3/4-inch thick; eggplant ½-inch thick. Have ready 3 shallow dishes:

(flour) + (beaten eggs) + [(wheat germ) or (fine bread crumbs)]   (Option: You can add a few dashes of basil, oregano or grated parmesan to the wheat germ/bread crumbs.)

Dip the slices in flour, then egg, then germ or crumbs. Fry in olive oil on each side until tender and brown (easily pierced with a fork.) Drain and proceed.   (Note: if you are averse to fried foods, the vegetables can be baked on lightly-oiled trays. About 20-25 minutes at 350°.)

For Parmesan

Grate 1 lb. mozzarella cheese (or slice it thinly), and enough parmesan cheese to make 1 cup.

In an oiled 9x13" pan, layer zucchini and/or eggplant with sauce and cheeses.

Bake 30-40 minutes, uncovered for last 15, at 375°. Let sit 10 minutes before serving.

For Lasagne

Follow lasagne recipe (p.124), substituting zucchini and/or eggplant for the Noodles.

Ode to Chang Kung

6 servings

½ hour to prepare

Chang Kung is the Chinese Kitchen God, who watches over your stove when you bring out your wok.

- 3 cups (raw) flat egg noodles, cooked in salted water; drained

- 3 stalks fresh broccoli, thinly sliced

- 1 large, sliced onion

- ½ lb. sliced fresh mushrooms

- 1 lb. fresh mung bean sprouts

- ½ cup each~ sliced water chestnuts & bamboo shoots

- ½ lb. Tofu (soybean curd), cut into small chunks (about 3 cakes)

- 2 Tbs. sesame oil

- 3 Tbs. safflower oil

- ¼ cup sherry

- ¼ cup tamari

- ½ tsp. freshly grated ginger (or more, to taste)

- ½ tsp. dry mustard

OPTIONAL
→ minced garlic, sautéed
→ black mushrooms, softened in boiling water, sliced & sautéed.
→ extra vegetables

Sauté onions, broccoli, ginger and mushrooms in safflower oil until tender. Add remaining ingredients; toss to mix and heat thoroughly. Top with toasted sesames and cashews, chopped scallions and green peppers.

VEGETABLE ST

40 minutes

2 medium onions, sliced
3 cloves crushed garlic
2 medium potatoes - in sm
3 carrots, sliced
2 stalks celery, sliced
1 eggplant, diced
2 medium-small zucchini, in chunks
1 stalk fresh broccoli, sliced
3 fresh tomatoes, diced
¼ lb. sliced mushrooms
3 Tbs. tomato paste
3 Tbs. molasses
1 tsp. dill weed
½ cup burgundy
salt and pepper
butter for sauté

butternut squ
face down,
to eat.

In a stew pot, begin sautéing onions, garlic, potatoes and eggplant in butter. Salt and pepper lightly. When potatoes begin to get tender, add celery, broccoli and carrots, along with burgundy. Steam until all vegetables begin to be tender, then add zucchini, tomato paste, mushrooms, molasses and dill. Cover and simmer over low heat about 20 minutes. Correct seasoning.

Serve piping hot, topped with
Sour Cream
and freshly-chopped parsley

STUFFED SQUASH

(acorn or butternut)

[f]our servings of stuffed squash, split 2 decent-sized acorn or
[squa]shes lengthwise down the middle. Remove the seeds and bake,
[o]n an oiled tray for 30 minutes at 350° – or, until tender enough
Make your choice of fillings while the squash is baking.

FILLING ONE:
Mushroom-Cheese

½ lb. chopped mushrooms / 1 cup chopped onion / 1 clove crushed garlic

1 cup cottage cheese / ½ tsp. basil / ¼ cup chopped parsley / salt, pepper

¾ cup bread crumbs or cooked rice / 2 Tbs. dry white wine / butter

Sauté mushrooms, onions and garlic in butter with salt and
pepper until onions are soft. Drain well (save liquid) and combine with
remaining ingredients. Fill the squash cavities amply and bake, uncovered
25-30 minutes at 350°. Baste with liquid from sauté while it bakes.

FILLING TWO:
Apple

2 medium cooking apples, chopped / 2 cups cottage cheese / juice from 1 lemon

½ cup chopped onion / 3 Tbs. butter / dash of cinnamon / ¾ cup grated cheddar

Sauté apples and onion in butter until onion is clear. Combine
with remaining ingredients and stuff the squash. Bake, covered, 15-20
minutes, or until heated through.

optional: ½ cup chopped walnuts (sautéed)
handful of raisins or currants

FILLING THREE:
Comprehensively - stuffed
(a good Thanksgiving main course
for vegetarians)

½ cup chopped onion

1 clove (large) crushed garlic

½ tsp. rubbed sage

½ tsp. thyme

3-4 Tbs. butter

1 cup coarsely-crumbled
 whole wheat bread

¼ cup chopped walnuts

¼ cup sunflower seeds

1 stalk chopped celery

juice from ½ lemon

¼ cup raisins (optional)

½ cup grated cheddar cheese

salt and pepper to taste

Sauté onions, garlic, celery, nuts and seeds (lightly-salted) in butter. Cook over low heat until onions are clear, nuts are browned, celery is tender. (in other words, cook until everything is perfect.) Add remaining ingredients, except cheese. Cook, stirring, over low heat 5-8 minutes - until everything is acquainted. Remove from heat and mix in the cheese. Pack stuffing into squash cavities. Bake, covered, at 350°, 25 minutes.   Serve with cranberry relish and/or:

.........A COLORFUL ACCOMPANIMENT:

4 servings

2 healthy Beets (the size of a healthy fist)

2 Tbs. butter for sauté

1 medium carrot (also in good health)

1 large clove crushed garlic

¾ cup orange juice

salt and pepper to taste

Peel and coarsely grate the beet and carrot. Cook the garlic gently in the butter for 2 minutes, then add the remaining ingredients. Cook, stirring, over medium heat 5-8 minutes. Season to taste.

129

Cauliflower~Cheese Pie

Preparation Time: about 2 hours, including baking

1 9-inch pie

(...with Grated Potato Crust)

Crust: 2 cups, packed, grated raw potato
         ½ tsp. salt
         1 egg, beaten
         ¼ cup grated onion   Heat oven to 400°.

    Set the freshly-grated potato in a colander over a bowl. Salt it and leave it for 10 minutes. Then squeeze out the excess water (which can be used for soup stock) and add it to the remaining ingredients. Pat it into a well-oiled 9-inch pie pan, building up the sides of the crust with lightly-floured fingers. Bake for 40-45 minutes – until browned. After the first 30 minutes brush the crust with a little oil to crispen it.

Turn oven down to 375°.

Filling: 1 heaping, packed cup grated cheddar cheese
           1 medium cauliflower, broken into small flowerets
           1 medium clove crushed garlic
           1 cup chopped onion
           3 Tbs. butter
           dash of thyme
           ½ tsp. basil
           ½ tsp. salt
           2 eggs
           ¼ cup milk   } beaten together
           black pepper
           paprika

    Sauté onions and garlic, lightly salted, in butter for 5 minutes. Add herbs and cauliflower and cook, covered, 10 minutes, stirring occasionally. Spread half the cheese into the baked crust, then the sauté, then the rest of the cheese. Pour the custard over and dust with paprika. Bake 35-40 minutes – until set.

130

Stuffed Zucchini, Turkish Style

One hour
to prepare and bake.

4 servings
(2 halves per serving)

4 medium zucchini (about 7" long), halved lengthwise

3 Tbs. butter

¾ cup finely-minced onion

3 smallish cloves crushed garlic

3 beaten eggs

½ cup crumbled feta cheese

¾ cup grated Swiss cheese

2 Tbs. freshly-chopped parsley

1 Tbs. fresh, chopped dill
(or, ¾ tsp. dried dill weed)

1½ Tbs. flour

salt and pepper to taste

paprika for the top

Scoop out the insides of the zucchini to leave a half-inch rim. Chop the innards into little bits and cook in butter with onions, garlic, salt (a few shakes) and pepper until onions are soft. Combine with flour, cheeses, herbs and beaten eggs. Correct salt and pepper. Fill the zucchini cavities and dust the tops with paprika. Bake at 375° 30 minutes, or until the filling solidifies. Serve with a fresh tomato salad.

Green Tomato Rellenos

...A variation of the famous Mexican Stuffed Vegetable. This recipe is exotic and time-consuming, but the product is delicious and well-worth the trouble. Gardeners whose tomatoes are not going to make it (we have early frosts in Ithaca, New York) will appreciate this outlet for their unripened fruit.

If you allow two medium tomatoes per person, plan on serving four persons from this recipe. Give yourself about two hours to prepare these.

Ⓐ

8 medium tomatoes (3" diameter)- Green and Firm, hollowed-out.

Use a grapefruit knife and the various ends of a teaspoon to create a cavity about the size and shape of a healthy golf ball. Save the insides for filling.

Ⓑ

Parboil the tomatoes, or roast them under a broiler, turning them, so that all sides get equal treatment. Cook until the tomato is tender (not mushy) and the skin is puckering. A fork should be insertable without too much resistance. Cool the tomatoes, and remove the skins carefully with a sharp paring knife.

THE FILLING:

minced green tomato innards
3/4 cup coarse bread crumbs (rye or onion bread are especially good.)
3/4 cup grated mild white cheese
2 Tbs. grated onion
2 medium cloves crushed garlic
1 tsp. ground cumin
several dashes of cayenne
salt and pepper to taste

Combine all the filling ingredients. Stuff the tomatoes delicately. Lightly dust the stuffed tomatoes with sifted flour.

THE BATTER:

① Separate 3 large eggs.

② Beat the whites until they form soft peaks.

③ Beat the yolks with 1 Tbs. water, 3 Tbs. flour and ¼ tsp. salt until thick and creamy.

④ Fold the yolks into the whites.

THE FRYING:

You can either pan-fry or deep-fry your Tomato Rellenos. In both cases you coat the stuffed tomato with the egg batter, and in both cases the tomatoes should be served shortly after frying. (Have a 300° oven pre-lit to keep them warm until all are fried.) If you pan-fry, you'll have a fluffy omelette-type coating around the tomato. If you deep-fry, you'll have a puffy, crispy fritter.

<u>To Pan-fry</u>: Heat several tablespoonsful of butter or oil in a large, heavy skillet. Spoon some batter in and place a tomato on top. Fry over medium heat about five minutes, then spoon more batter on top and turn it. Fry until evenly coated and browned.

<u>To Deep-fry</u>: It is important that the oil be hot enough when the tomatoes go in. Start heating a 2½-3 inch pool of vegetable oil or processed peanut oil ("natural" oils tend to froth) about ten minutes ahead of time. When you're ready to fry, test the temperature of the oil by flicking in a drop of the batter. The batter must sizzle and puff up immediately upon contact, or the oil isn't hot enough. If you have a kitchen thermometer, the mercury should hit 360°.

Use a large spoon to dunk each tomato into the batter and lift it out, bringing a coating of batter with it. Drop the whole spoonful into the hot oil and fry until puffy and brown. Drain well on a pile of paper towels, and keep warm until ready to serve.

Arabian Squash-Cheese Casserole

1¾ - 2 hours' preparation time

4 servings
375° oven

2 medium-large butternut or
   acorn squash

1 heaping cup chopped onion

2-3 cloves crushed garlic

1 heaping cup mixed green and
   red peppers, chopped

3 Tbs. butter for sauté

1 tsp. salt

black and red pepper to taste

(¼ cup sunflower seeds or
   chopped nuts, for the
   top.)

2 beaten eggs

1 cup buttermilk or yogurt

1 cup crumbled feta cheese

Cut the squash down the middle, lengthwise. Scoop out the seeds, and place it face-down on an oiled tray. Bake it at 375° about 35 minutes, or until soft. Cool until handle-able; scoop out and mash.

Sauté the onion and garlic, lightly-salted, in butter. When the onion is translucent add the chopped peppers. Sauté until peppers are just under-done.

Beat eggs with buttermilk or yogurt. Crumble in the feta cheese. Combine everything and mix well. Add salt, black pepper and red pepper or hot sauce to taste.

Spread into buttered casserole or baking pan. Top with seeds or nuts.
Bake at 375° . . . . . . covered, 25 minutes.
                        uncovered, 10 minutes.

Szechwan Eggplant & Tofu

1½ hours to prepare

Szechwan is the spiciest of Chinese cuisines. This is a stir-fry dish, which means you should have your ingredients prepared and assembled when your dinner guests arrive, so you can fry and serve immediately. Your rice should be a little more than half-done when frying begins. (Start about 2½ cups raw rice in 4½ cups boiling water about 10-15 minutes before frying.)

About some of the exotic ingredients in this recipe: "tree ears" are a dried fungus, related to mushrooms. They are sold in little ounce-packets in oriental food stores. Szechwan pepper is not always easy to find, but if you find some, prepare it by dry-roasting in a skillet until it smokes lightly, giving off an incense-like aroma. Then remove from heat and grind it in a spice grinder or with mortar and pestle. If you can't get it, black pepper will do.

3 Tbs. soy or safflower oil
½ cup thinly-sliced onion
8 scallions (greens minced, bottoms cut into strips)
1 Tbs. freshly-minced garlic
1 tsp. freshly-grated ginger
¼ tsp. freshly-ground anise
1 large eggplant, cut into strips:

(thin slices lengthwise, then strips, cut across)
(7-8 cups of strips)

4 cakes fresh tofu (bean curd) cut into chunks
½ oz. tree ears (soaked in boiling water until soft; then sliced)
½ tsp. salt
¼ tsp. (or more) ground black or Szechwan pepper
¼ tsp. cayenne pepper

3 Tbs. tamari
3 Tbs. sherry   } plus enough
1 tsp. sugar   water to make
1 tsp. dark vinegar}   1 cup

3 Tbs. cornstarch

Heat oil in wok or large, heavy skillet. Add onions, garlic and salt. Stir-fry 5 minutes. Add ginger and fry 5 more minutes. Add eggplant and stir fry over fairly high flame until eggplant begins to wilt (about 8-10 minutes). Add anise, tofu, tree ears and pepper.

Whisk the tamari-liquid mixture into the cornstarch until you have a smooth substance. Add to the eggplant, mix well, and cover. Lower the heat and let sit about 5 minutes. Then, uncover, raise heat back to medium, and stir-fry until the eggplant is very tender. Toss in scallion bottoms (in strips) just before removing from the heat. Sprinkle scallion greens on top of each serving.

135

సత్యమ్మ ప్రసిద్ధి గోపి ఉప్పుర కూర
(Satyamma's Famous Cauliflower Curry)

40 minutes
  to prepare

4-6 servings

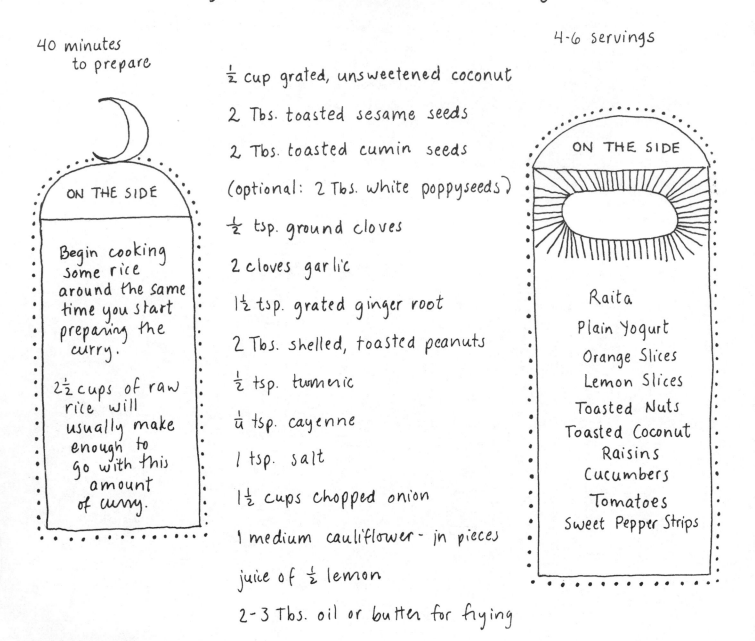

ON THE SIDE

Begin cooking some rice around the same time you start preparing the curry.

2½ cups of raw rice will usually make enough to go with this amount of curry.

½ cup grated, unsweetened coconut

2 Tbs. toasted sesame seeds

2 Tbs. toasted cumin seeds

(optional: 2 Tbs. white poppyseeds)

½ tsp. ground cloves

2 cloves garlic

1½ tsp. grated ginger root

2 Tbs. shelled, toasted peanuts

½ tsp. turmeric

¼ tsp. cayenne

1 tsp. salt

1½ cups chopped onion

1 medium cauliflower - in pieces

juice of ½ lemon

2-3 Tbs. oil or butter for frying

ON THE SIDE

Raita
Plain Yogurt
Orange Slices
Lemon Slices
Toasted Nuts
Toasted Coconut
Raisins
Cucumbers
Tomatoes
Sweet Pepper Strips

* Pureé in blender 1st ten ingredients (add enough water so blender can work) until reduced to a homogeneous mixture.

* Fry the onions until translucent. Add cauliflower and mix. Add salt.

* Add blended mixture and cook (covered, low heat) until cauliflower is tender, stirring every several minutes. Additional water might be necessary. (or orange juice.)

* Add lemon juice and cook a few minutes more. Adjust for salt.

Vegetable-Almond Medley

1½ hours to prepare
400° oven

6 servings

3 lbs. mixed vegetables (your favorites) - (or, about 4-5 cups, chopped)

1 cup chopped onion
2 medium cloves minced garlic
1 cup chopped almonds
2 cups water
5 Tbs. butter
3 Tbs. flour

1 tsp. prepared horseradish
dash or two of tabasco sauce
½ tsp. dry mustard
1 Tbs. tamari
salt and pepper to taste

topping { ½ cup chopped, toasted almonds
{ ½ cup fine breadcrumbs

① Sauté onions and garlic in 2 Tbs. butter, salting them lightly. When onions are translucent add vegetables. Add the longer-cooking vegetables (cabbage, broccoli, cauliflower, carrots, celery) first and softer vegies (zucchini, peppers, mushrooms) later. Sauté until all are cooked to your liking.

② Toast 1 cup chopped almonds. Place in blender with water. Purée until smooth. This is "almond milk."

③ Melt 3 Tbs. butter and whisk in 3 Tbs. flour. Add almond milk and seasonings, stirring constantly over low heat. Simmer for 10 minutes, or until thickened. (Stir occasionally during simmering.)

④ Combine sautéed vegetables with almond sauce. Add salt and pepper to taste. Pour into a large, buttered casserole. Sprinkle with combined breadcrumbs and chopped, toasted almonds.

⑤ Bake, uncovered, at 400° 15 minutes.

Note: You can use cashews instead of, or in addition to, almonds. But don't use walnuts. They might make it turn purple and taste bitter. (unless you happen to have a penchant for bitter, purple casseroles.)

Cossack Pie

Approximately 2 hours'
preparation time

- preheat oven to 350°
- one 9-inch pie

1 unbaked 9-inch pie crust

¼ lb. fresh mushrooms

1 cup chopped onions

1 cup shredded green cabbage

1 cup thinly-sliced broccoli

1 cup thinly-sliced carrot

1 finely-chopped scallion

salt and fresh, black pepper

3 Tbs. butter

paprika

2 Tbs. flour

½ tsp. ground caraway seed

½ tsp. basil

2 Tbs. dry white wine

½ tsp. dill weed

⅓ cup pot, farmer's or
        cottage cheese

2 eggs

¾ cup mixed sour cream
        and yogurt

(1) Remove stems from mushrooms. Slice caps and set aside. Chop stems finely. (Include the chopped stems, not the caps, in step 2.)

(2) In butter - sauté all the vegetables except the scallion until just tender. Salt them lightly as they sauté. Add spices. Remove from heat and toss with flour and wine.

(3) Purée the eggs and cheese together in a blender. Add salt + pepper.

(4) Add egg-cheese purée to sautéed vegetables, along with the chopped, raw scallion. Mix well. Spread into crust.

(5) Sauté the sliced mushroom caps in a little butter—about 5 minutes.

(6) Spread the sour cream-yogurt mixture on top of the vegetable filling. Arrange the mushroom caps on top, gently. Dust with paprika.

Bake 40 minutes, or until set, at 350°.

Let stand 10 minutes before serving.

Solyanka

Approximately 1¼ hours' preparation time, including baking.

Preheat oven to 350°.

~ a hearty vegetable-cheese casserole, this makes a lovely main dish when accompanied by cucumber salad. This recipe should satisfy 4-6 healthy appetites.

4 medium potatoes

4 packed cups shredded green cabbage

1½ cups chopped onion

3 Tbs. butter

½ tsp. ground caraway seed

½ tsp. dill weed

¼ cup sunflower seeds

1½ cups cottage cheese

1½ tsp. salt

black pepper

paprika

½ cup sour cream

½ cup yogurt

2 Tbs. cider vinegar

Scrub (don't peel) the potatoes. Cut them into small pieces and boil until mashable. Drain and mash, while still hot, with cottage cheese, sour cream and yogurt. Sauté onions in butter with ½ tsp. salt. After 5 minutes add ground caraway, cabbage and remaining salt. Sauté until cabbage is tender. Combine with potato mixture, and add everything except 2 Tbs. sunflower seeds and paprika. Taste to correct seasoning.

Spread into a deep, buttered casserole. Top with paprika and remaining sunflower seeds. Bake at 350°, uncovered, 35-40 minutes.

Felafel

From the cuisine
of Israel
... spicy chickpea
croquettes,
deep-fried, and
served in pocket
bread with salad
and tahini sauce.

Begin soaking
2 cups raw chickpeas
about 4 hours
before assembling.

Batter only takes
a few minutes to
assemble, but needs
one hour to chill.

If you choose to make
your own pocket bread
(there's a recipe in
"Miscellaneous Baked Things"
chapter) - do it early
in the morning. Or - you
can buy it at most
grocery stores.

6 servings
(several felafel
per sandwich)

4 cups cooked chickpeas (2 cups, soaked
1½ hours, boiled until very soft, drained)

3 medium cloves crushed garlic

½ cup each (finely-minced) — celery
— scallions

½ tsp. ground cumin

½ tsp. turmeric

(extra flour
for coating)

2 beaten eggs

3 Tbs. tahini

3 Tbs. flour or
fine bread crumbs

¼ tsp. cayenne; dash of black pepper

1½ tsp. salt (more, to taste)

Mash the chickpeas well (make sure you cook them well enough to be mashable.) Combine with other ingredients. Chill well. With floured hands make the batter into one-inch-diameter balls. Dust each one lightly with flour. Heat a 2-inch pool of oil in a heavy skillet to 365°. Deep-fry the felafel until golden, and serve immediately.

NOTE: While the felafel batter chills, prepare tahini-lemon sauce (see sauce chapter) and a salad of diced cucumbers, tomatoes and peppers. Douse the salad with plain oil and vinegar. Serve in pocket bread, all piled together. (You can warm the bread in the oven while the felafel fries.)

Scheherezade Casserole

- Ground soybeans with bulghar give this dish heartiness and a perfectly-balanced protein. Vegetables, spices and feta cheese lend a full and provocative flavor.

Soybeans need about 4 hours to soak.
Preparation + Baking times = about 1½ hours

6 servings
375° oven

¾ cup raw soybeans, soaked in lots of water for at least 4 hours

1 cup raw bulghar, soaked 15 minutes in 1 cup boiling water

2 medium green peppers, chopped

4 medium-sized fresh tomatoes, chopped

1½ cups chopped onion   2 cloves crushed garlic

¼ cup freshly-chopped parsley   salt, pepper, tabasco to taste

3 Tbs. tomato paste   1 tsp. ground cumin

1½ cups crumbled feta   1 tsp. basil

① Place soaked soybeans in the blender jar with 1½ cups water. Purée.
② Combine puréed soybeans and soaked bulghar.

③ Sauté the onions and garlic in a little oil, lightly-salted. When soft, add peppers. Sauté 5 minutes.

④ Combine all ingredients except feta. Place in a large, buttered casserole. Sprinkle feta on top.

⑤ Bake one hour at 375° (covered, first 45 minutes, uncovered, last 15)

Eggplant Curry

30 minutes to prepare.

Start cooking your rice when you start to prepare the curry.

About 2½ cups raw rice should be enough for this amount of curry.

[4-5 servings]

1½ tsp. mustard seeds
   (black or yellow)

1 tsp. sesame seeds

1½ cups chopped onion

1 tsp. salt

1 tsp. turmeric

dash of cayenne

6 cups cubed eggplant
   (1-inch cubes)

1 Tbs. fresh coriander leaves,
   minced

2 Tbs. oil or butter

1½ cups sweet, green peas,
   steamed until bright green

① Heat oil or butter in a large, heavy skillet. Add seeds.

② When seeds start to pop, add onion, salt, turmeric, cayenne. Cook, stirring until onion is translucent.

③ Add eggplant. Cook, stirring regularly, about 15 minutes. (until eggplant is soft, but pieces still separate and whole.) Additional oil or a little water might be needed, if mixture is too dry.

④ Add half the fresh coriander and cook 2-3 minutes.

⑤ Serve immediately, topped with remaining coriander and adorned with bright green peas.

This is good with Cucumber Raita (in "sauces" chapter).

REFRITOS
(REFRIED BEANS)

Begin to soak the beans at least 3 hours before you need them.

This recipe yields 4-6 servings, depending on how you serve them.

2 cups raw pinto beans

1½ tsp. salt

1½ cups chopped onion

3 cloves crushed garlic

½ cup minced green pepper

optional: ¼ tsp. coriander

2 tsp. ground cumin

olive oil (about 3 Tbs.)

¼ tsp. black pepper

Cover the pintos with water and let soak 1½ hours or more. Cover with more water and cook, partially-covered, until well-done - usually 1½-2 hours. Make sure you check their water level periodically while they cook. When they are soft, drain off excess water and mash them well with a wooden pestle or a potato-masher.

Heat about 3 Tbs. olive oil in a skillet. Add onions, garlic, cumin and ½ tsp. salt. Cook over low heat until onions are translucent. Add green pepper, cover, and simmer 5-8 minutes. Add sautéed vegetables to the beans, along with 1 tsp. salt and black pepper. Mix well. Keep the beans hot in a medium oven until ready to serve.

Serve in tostadas, stuffed into green pepper halves + baked, or, for a simple and authentic Mexican dinner, with plain cooked rice and steamed tortillas. These beans (especially when stuffed into peppers) love <u>Nachos Sauce</u>.

143

TOSTADAS

An all-day project.   6 servings

A tostada is an open-faced, multi-layered Mexican sandwich to end all sandwiches. The different layers create contrasts of color, texture and flavor, which are beautiful-looking and tasting.

Invite your friends over for a tostada-building party. Spread a large table with dishes of tostada accessories, and do it smorgasbord-style.

Things to prepare in advance:

① HOT SAUCE - (recipe in Sauce chapter) Begin your hot sauce in the morning. Let it simmer slowly for several hours. One batch is plenty for six hungry persons eating two tostadas a piece.

② REFRIED BEANS- (recipe on preceeding page) Begin soaking your beans about five hours before serving time. Again, one batch is ample for six enthusiastic sorts.

③ DEEP-FRIED TORTILLAS - There are usually a dozen per package – or make your own. (recipe in "Miscellaneous Baked Things" chapter.) Fry until crisp in a one-inch pool of thoroughly preheated (365°) oil. Drain well on paper towels. Pile into a bread basket lined with paper towels. These will keep all day. You can fry them up in the morning.

④ ACCESSORIES - pick and choose your favorite toppings. Arrange them in little bowls here and there in your tostada studio:

★ chopped olives

★ chopped hard-cooked egg

★ chopped sweet, pickled peppers or pimientos

★ grated mild, white cheese

★ very, very finely (chairlike) shredded cabbage

★ shredded lettuce

★ sliced avocadoes

★ chopped tomatoes

★ sour cream

Keep beans and hot sauce warm in chafing dishes or fondue pots.

★ ★
★ ★
★ ★

How to Eat a Tostada:

Take a tortilla. Put it on
your plate. Cover it with refried
beans, spreading them imaginatively into place.
Sprinkle on some grated cheese. It will melt onto
your beans. Yum yum. Arrange handsful of olives,
pickled peppers, shredded cabbage, chopped eggs and
tomatoes in a pile the height of which considers the
dimensions of your mouth. Ladle on some hot sauce
and a hunk of sour cream.

Eat it sitting down, holding the plate under your chin to pick up
what drops as you progress from one end of the tostada to the other. If you
need two hands to eat it, find a trusted friend to hold up your plate for you.

145

Zucchini-Feta Pancakes

One usually thinks of a pancake supper as a generally-starchy affair. However, the bulk of these lovely pancakes consists of eggs and zucchini- with just enough flour to bind them.

This makes enough to comfortably fill four average-sized persons.

About 30 minutes to prepare, before frying.

4 packed cups coarsely grated zucchini
4 eggs, separated
1 heaping cup finely-crumbled feta cheese
½ cup minced scallions
3/4 tsp. dried mint
salt and black pepper
⅓ cup flour

butter for frying
sour cream or yogurt for topping

Place the grated zucchini in a colander in a bowl, salt it lightly and let it stand 15 minutes. Rinse it, and squeeze out all excess water.

Combine squeezed zucchini, egg yolks, feta, scallions, flour, and spices. Mix well.

Beat the eggwhites until they form soft peaks. Fold into first mixture.

Fry in butter, on both sides, until golden and crisp. Serve topped with sour cream or yogurt.

Apple-Cheese Pancakes

Serve these pancakes for breakfast, brunch or lunch. They could even be a dessert after a light meal.

This recipe makes enough to satisfy four reasonably hungry sorts.

1 cup cottage or ricotta cheese

1 heaping, packed cup grated apple
   (any kind but delicious)

3/4 cup flour (you can use ½ cup white
   and ¼ cup whole wheat)

1 Tbs. honey

1 tsp. fresh lemon juice

1 Tbs. sunflower seeds or chopped almonds

½ tsp. cinnamon

dash of nutmeg or all spice

4 eggs, separated

½ tsp. salt

Mix everything together except eggwhites. Beat these until stiff and fold into batter. Fry pancakes in butter on both sides until brown.

Serve with maple syrup or preserves, sour cream or yogurt, fresh fruit, cinnamon sugar. (Mix and match.)

Fresh Vegetable Sauté

One of the most popular meals at Moosewood is also one of the simplest: freshly-sautéed vegetables over grains. Sometimes there'll be a sauce drizzled on top; other times the sauté will be seasoned with just one or two herbs and tamari sauce.

Any combination of vegetables can be used for sauté. We usually use onions, carrots, cabbage, broccoli, cauliflower, zucchini, peppers, mushrooms and celery. Thin strips of sweet potato or winter squash add color, and whole green beans add texture. Use whatever is available to you. Plan on approximately 2½ cups of cut, raw vegies per serving - remember that many vegetables shrink from water loss during cooking, thus decreasing in volume.

Cook your grains ahead of time. Three cups raw should feed six. Rice needs about 25 minutes and 4½-5 cups water. Millet, in 5½ cups water, needs about 15 minutes. Three cups bulghar needs to soak, not cook, in twice as much boiling water, about 15-20 minutes.

Prepare your sauce ahead of time. Keep it warm while you cook grains and prepare vegetables. Choose any appropriate, appealing sauce from the "Sauces" chapter -or- serve plain, sauceless sauté. Choose a couple of herbs instead (thyme and marjoram ..... dill and tarragon ...... basil and oregano.....)

Cut the vegetables into bite-sized pieces and on the thin side. This way they will cook quickly and retain color, crispness and nutrients. Separate cut vegetables into three groups: ① onions ② Harder, longer-cooking types (carrots, celery, cabbage, cauliflower, green beans, broccoli). ③ Softer, quick-cookers: zucchini, mushrooms, peppers. If you use spinach keep it separate and add it last. This separation method allows each vegetable no more than Just Enough Time, preventing mushiness.

Use a heavy skillet. Heat a small amount of safflower or peanut oil. Add onions, a little salt, and herbs. Sauté until onions are soft. Then add group ② and sauté until tender, then add group ③. Keep heat at medium. Stir as you sauté.

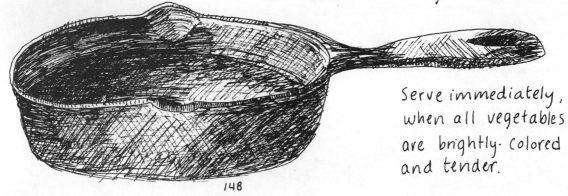

Serve immediately, when all vegetables are brightly-colored and tender.

Sauté, Chinese-Style

Make a batch of tamari-ginger sauce. (the recipe is in the "sauces" section of this book.) Place 2 tablespoons of cornstarch in a small bowl. Add a little of the tamari-ginger sauce and mix well to form a smooth and uniform paste. Return the paste to the sauce, and whisk well until the sauce takes on a cloud-like appearance.

Meanwhile, prepare your vegetables for sauté and your rice in the usual fashion.

In addition, or in partial substitution, you may choose:

All of these, except the Bok choy greens and the mung sprouts, are "hard" vegetables.

- Bok choy   (a fresh vegetable, sold in some supermarkets and in many oriental food shops. It resembles a cross between celery and swiss chard. Use both stems (sliced thinly) and leaves.
- Chinese cabbage
- Thinly-sliced water chestnuts and bamboo shoots
- Fresh mung bean sprouts
- Soaked, drained, and thinly-sliced black mushrooms

Halfway through the cooking of the hard vegetables, whisk the tamari-ginger sauce from the bottom—to stir up the cornstarch—and add it directly to the sauté. Keep stirring throughout the remaining cooking. The sauce will coat the vegetables and make them shine.

Serve over rice, topped with scallions and sesame seeds.

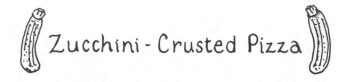 Zucchini-Crusted Pizza

4-6 servings

A normal pizza on top, and a beautiful egg-and-cheese crust, with flecks of green and a slight crunch.

Preheat oven to 350°.

The Crust
{
- 3½ cups grated zucchini (grate it coarsely)
- 3 eggs, beaten
- ⅓ cup flour
- ½ cup grated mozzarella
- ½ cup grated parmesan
- 1 Tbs. fresh basil leaves, minced (if you don't have fresh basil, use ½ tsp. dried)

salt and pepper

Salt the zucchini lightly and let it sit for 15 minutes. Squeeze out all the excess moisture.

Combine all crust ingredients, and spread into an oiled 9x13-inch baking pan. Bake 20-25 minutes- until the surface is dry and firm. Brush the top with oil and broil it, under moderate heat for 5 minutes.

Pile all of your favorite pizza toppings on (tomato sauce, olives, sautéed mushrooms, strips of peppers, lots of cheese -etc.), and heat the whole mess in a 350° oven for about 25 minutes. Serve hot, cut into squares, with a big tossed salad.

Spanakopita

~ a Greek spinach pastry ~

1½ hours' preparation time

8 servings

375° oven

2 cups crumbled feta cheese   5 eggs
2 Tbs. flour   3 Tbs. butter
1 cup chopped onion   1 tsp. basil   salt, pepper
2 cups (1 lb.) cottage or pot cheese   ½ tsp. oregano
2 lbs. fresh spinach

Clean, stem and chop the spinach. Salt it lightly, and cook, adding no water, for five minutes.

Cook the onions in butter, salting lightly. When soft, combine with remaining ingredients and spinach.

. . . .

To Assemble:

Have on hand —

> a 1-lb. package defrosted filo dough
> ½ lb. melted butter

Spread melted butter on a 9x13" baking pan. Place a strüdel leaf in the pan (it will outsize the pan. Let the edges climb the sides.) and brush generously with butter. Keep layers of dough coming, one on top of another, brushing each with butter. When you have a pile of 8 leaves, spread on half the filling. Continue with another stack of 8 or so leaves (don't skimp on the butter), then apply the remaining filling, spreading it to the edges. Fold the excess filo down along the edges, making little tidy corners.

Pile as many more layers of filo and butter as your baking pan will accommodate. Butter the top-most leaf and sprinkle with a Tablespoonful of whole anise or fennel seeds, if you have some on hand.

Bake uncovered, about 45 minutes - till golden.

TEMPURA VEGETABLES

(Japanese-style batter-fried vegetables)

A tempura meal consists of batter-fried vegetables (and fruit), rice, and tamari-ginger sauce for dipping the tempura. (There's a recipe for tamari-ginger sauce in the "sauces" chapter of this book.) You can use any combination of vegetables ~ broccoli flowerets, onion slices, carrot slices, cauliflowerets, whole mushroom caps, green beans, green pepper strips, sweet potato slices- etcetera. Slices of apple and banana go very well too. For each serving of tempura, figure on at least ten chunks of fried whatever (you can do shrimps and 1-inch pieces of fish as well.). Have your rice cooked in advance, and start your oil heating about 10 minutes before you plan to fry. And, of course, be sure the tamari-ginger sauce is all put-together too. Cut (or break, as in the case of cauliflower) the vegetables into small pieces or thin slices. Green beans can be left whole.

Tempura Batter: (for 6 servings'-worth of tidbits)

2½ cups sifted flour   2 cups cold water

3 egg yolks   dash of salt   (oil for frying- 3-4 cups)

Beat the egg yolks with the water. When the mixture is smooth, sift in the pre-sifted flour gradually, stirring as you go. Stir only until batter is combined.

The oil should be at least 325°F and not more than 350°F. Dip the ingredients in the batter and carefully drop them into the oil. Fry until brown and puffy and risen to the surface.
Drain on paper towels and either serve immediately, or keep warm in a 300° oven- on a tray, in a single layer.

PAKORA VEGETABLES

(Indian-style batter-fried vegetables)

Pakora is basically the same idea as tempura, so read the tempura recipe to get the method down. The pakora batter is different, and pakora vegetables get a different sauce, but you can use the same vegetables, cutting-style and frying technique.

Serve Pakora with rice, chutney and raita (recipes for both chutney and raita can be found in the "sauces" section of this book.)

The Pakora batter calls for chickpea flour. You might have to shop around for this item. Check out imported foods sections of grocery stores, oriental food shops, natural food stores. Don't substitute any other kind of flour. The flavor of chickpea flour (and its texture) are inimitable.

Here is a recipe for your spicy Pakora batter:

(enough for 6 people)

1½ cups chickpea flour
1½ tsp. salt
½ tsp. cayenne
1½ tsp. turmeric
½ tsp. ground cumin
1½ cups water

Mix together the dry ingredients first. Add about half the water, whisking. Gradually, as you whisk, add remaining water. Beat until all dry lumps are mixed in. Proceed with coating and frying vegetable and fruit tidbits, as described on preceding page.

Cheese-Beans

6 servings

Preheat oven to 350°.

→ Begin soaking 3 cups raw beans at least 3½ hours before you plan to Assemble.

An elegant-yet-simple, hearty Casserole with a difference.

Actually,
        with several differences.

6 cups cooked (3 cups raw) pinto or kidney beans

2 cups chopped onion   2 large cooking apples, in chunks

2 cups grated mild, white cheese
(muenster or Monterey Jack are best)

4 medium-sized fresh-chopped tomatoes   6 Tbs. dry white wine

2 tsp. chili powder   1 tsp. dry mustard

salt (about 1½ tsp.) and pepper

Clean the beans and soak them at least 1½ hours (use a large container so they'll have room to expand. Give them plenty of water). Cook them in lots of water, partially covered, about 1½ hours more, or until Done Enough For You. Drain off excess water. (This can be saved for soup, if you are so inclined.)

Sauté the onion in a little butter until it is soft and clear. Add chili powder and mustard. Combine cooked beans (make sure they are cooked enough. They won't soften much more as they bake.) with sautéed onions and all remaining ingredients. Pour into large buttered casserole. Cover and bake at 350° 35-40 minutes.   Serve with fresh corn bread. (They can bake together.)

SAMOSAS

One hour to prepare (before frying)   4 or 5 servings

These are turnovers with a yogurt pastry and a curried vegetable filling. They are deep-fried until golden and crisp, and served immediately. You can assemble them several hours in advance, storing them in refrigeration until frying time. Serve them with chutney and plenty of raita (both of these in Sauce chapter) and chunks of fresh, raw fruits and vegetables.

FILLING:

2 large potatoes, cooked and mashed
1 cup finely-minced onion
2 medium cloves crushed garlic
½ tsp. fresh-grated ginger root
½ tsp. mustard seeds
½ tsp. ground coriander
½ cup diced carrots, cooked until just tender
½ cup cooked green peas   (cayenne pepper to taste.)
1 tsp. salt
juice from ½ lemon
2-3 Tbs. butter

Heat butter in heavy skillet. Add garlic, ginger, onion, salt and mustard seeds. Saute 6-8 minutes, or until onion is soft and clear. Combine all ingredients, except peas, and mix well. Fold in peas last, taking care not to smash them.

PASTRY and PROCEDURE:

2 cups white flour
1 tsp. salt
4 Tbs. melted butter
⅓ cup yogurt
water

Sift together flour and salt. Add melted butter, yogurt, and enough water to make a stiff dough. Knead until smooth and elastic. Roll out very thin (¼-inch) on a floured board and cut into 4-inch circles. Keep rolling and cutting until you've used all the Dough. Place a Tbs. of filling (approximately... You might be able to fit more in.) in the center of each circle, leaving edges free. Brush edges with a little water, fold over, and seal with a fork.
    Heat a 3-inch pool of "all-purpose" or peanut oil in a heavy skillet to about 365°. Make sure the oil is hot enough (it should bounce a drop of water on contact.) Fry samosas until golden. Drain well and serve.

Eggplant-Almond Enchiladas

6 servings
(2 enchiladas per serving)

    Begin a batch of hot sauce (in sauce chapter) early in the day. Begin the enchiladas about 2½ hours before you plan to serve them. The enchilada filling is pre-cooked, the tortillas are pre-fried, and after you assemble them, they bake in a hot sauce bath. You can use store-bought, frozen tortillas or make your own (in "miscellaneous baked things" section). If you make your own, plan to spend most of the day on your enchilada project. It will be worth it!

Twelve Tortillas

6 cups cubed eggplant (approximately two small ones)
(not <u>teeny</u>, just modestly-proportioned)

1 cup chopped onion

2 medium cloves crushed garlic

1 cup chopped green pepper

1½ tsp. salt

lots of black pepper

1 packed cup grated mild, white cheese
(Monterey Jack or Brick are best)

1 cup chopped, toasted almonds

Vegetable oil for frying tortillas

2-3 Tbs. olive oil for sautéeing vegetables

Part One:

In a large skillet, begin sautéeing onions and garlic. Add salt. Cook, stirring occasionally, over medium heat for about five minutes.

Add the eggplant (which should be in ½-inch cubes). Mix. Cover and cook about ten minutes, or until eggplant is soft.

Add peppers, almonds and black pepper. Cook another five minutes, stirring frequently. Remove from heat and add cheese. Mix.

Part Two

Heat about one-half inch of vegetable oil in a heavy skillet. (Cast iron is best.) Fry each tortilla on both sides - only <u>Ten Seconds</u> on each side. (Don't fry them long enough to crispen or they'll break when you try to roll them up!) Drain them on paper towels.

Part Three

Fill each tortilla by placing a hunk (more or less ¼ cup) of filling on one side and rolling it up.

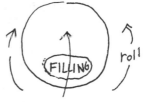

Situate your filled enchiladas gently in a baking pan. Pour your batch of hot sauce over the top. Heat in a 350° oven about 20 minutes.

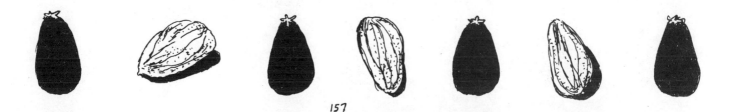

SPAGHETTI SQUASH

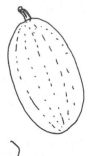

(... oval-shaped, about
4 inches in diameter,
about 8 inches long, a
light yellow-green color...)

Also known as "vegetable spaghetti", this summer squash baffles
many people who grow it or buy it, then take it to their kitchens and wonder
what to do next. It is not like zucchini, nor is it like winter squash. Once baked
or boiled, the insides of this strange vegetable are strand-like: the size and
shape of spaghetti, but with a slightly crunchy, delightful texture. The flavor is
buttery and slightly sweet. You can serve it topped with tomato sauce and cheese,
as you would regular spaghetti (it isn't starchy!) – or, you can build a casserole.
Here is a recipe for a Spaghetti Squash Casserole:

1½ hours to prepare   4-6 servings

1 8-inch spaghetti squash
1 cup chopped onion
2 medium cloves crushed garlic
2 fresh tomatoes (medium-sized)
½ lb. fresh, sliced mushrooms
½ tsp. oregano
salt and pepper   Butter for sauté.
1 cup cottage or ricotta cheese
1 cup grated mozzarella   Parmesan for the top.
¼ cup freshly-chopped parsley
1 tsp. basil
dash of thyme
1 cup fine bread crumbs.

Preheat oven to 375°.

Slice the squash in half lengthwise and scoop out the seeds. Bake it, face-
down, on a buttered tray at 375° for about 30 minutes, or until easily pierced
by a fork. Cool until handleable. Scoop out insides.

While the squash bakes, sauté the onions and garlic with salt, pepper, mushrooms &
herbs. When onions are soft, add freshly-chopped tomatoes. Cook until most of
the liquid evaporates.

Combine all ingredients. Pour into buttered 2-quart casserole. Top with lots
of grated parmesan. Bake at 375°, uncovered, about 40 minutes.

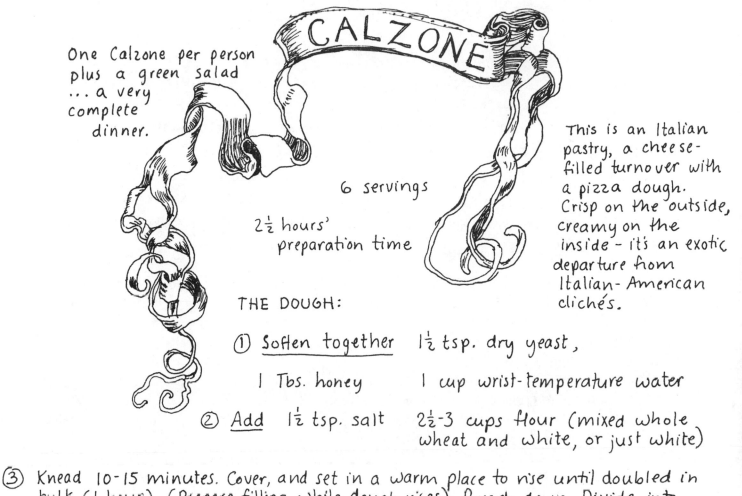

CALZONE

One Calzone per person plus a green salad ...a very complete dinner.

This is an Italian pastry, a cheese-filled turnover with a pizza dough. Crisp on the outside, creamy on the inside - it's an exotic departure from Italian-American clichés.

6 servings

2½ hours' preparation time

THE DOUGH:

① **Soften together**   1½ tsp. dry yeast,

     1 Tbs. honey   1 cup wrist-temperature water

② **Add**   1½ tsp. salt   2½-3 cups flour (mixed whole wheat and white, or just white)

③ Knead 10-15 minutes. Cover, and set in a warm place to rise until doubled in bulk (1 hour). (Prepare filling while dough rises.) Punch down. Divide into six sections and roll out in rounds ¼-inch thick. Fill with ½-¾ cup filling, placing filling on one half of the circle, leaving a ½ inch rim.

—filling   Moisten the rim with water, fold the empty side over, and crimp the edge with your favorite fork. Prick it here and there.
     Bake on an oiled tray in a pre-heated 450° oven for 15-20 minutes, or until crisp and lightly-browned. Brush each pastry with a little butter as it emerges from the oven.

THE FILLING:
1 lb. ricotta cheese
2 cloves crushed garlic / ½ cup minced onion
1 lb. fresh spinach / 2 packed cups grated mozzarella / salt, pepper
½ cup freshly-grated parmesan / dash of nutmeg
2 Tbs. butter

① Wash, stem, and finely-chop spinach. Steam it quickly, on medium-high heat, adding no additional water. When wilted and deep green, it is done and should be removed to mixing bowl with slotted spoon.

② Sauté onion and garlic in butter until translucent and soft.

③ Combine all ingredients, mix well, salt and pepper to taste.

CHEESE STRUDEL

Strudel, although most commonly thought of as dessert, can also be a main dish for brunch, lunch or dinner. These cheese strudels work beautifully as appetizers too.

It is very difficult and time-consuming to make strudel dough from scratch. Store-bought, prepackaged strudel dough (often labeled "Greek Filo Leaves") tastes just as good, and it saves much trouble. Buy it frozen, in one-pound packages. ALWAYS DEFROST IT STILL-WRAPPED! Strudel dough dries out quickly, becoming brittle and useless. Make the filling while the filo defrosts, and only unwrap the dough just before assembling.

One one-pound package of filo makes approximately 12 portions of strudel. (main-dish-sized) You can use half the dough and re-wrap and re-refrigerate the other half. Just be careful not to let it dry out. You can also make more strudel than you need, bake it all, and freeze some. It freezes and re-heats very well.

Here are recipes for two cheese strudel fillings. Each makes enough to fill two rolls (three servings per roll.) These two happen to go well together, for a mixed-strudel dinner or brunch.

CHEESE-RICE FILLING

3 cups cooked brown rice
(1½ cups raw in 2½ cups water)
1 heaping cup chopped onion
2 Tbs. butter
2 Tbs. sesame seeds
3 cups grated cheddar

Sauté onion in butter until soft and translucent.

Add sesame seeds. Toss and cook for about one minute.

Combine all ingredients. Add salt and pepper to taste.

BROCCOLI-CHEESE FILLING

6 cups raw, chopped broccoli
3 Tbs. butter
2 eggs, beaten
1 cup chopped onion
2 cups good bread crumbs
2 cups grated cheddar
juice from one lemon

salt and pepper

Sauté onion in butter with ½ tsp. salt. When onion is soft, add the broccoli. Salt lightly again, and sauté until broccoli is tender, but still bright green. (About 8 minutes over medium heat.)

Combine all ingredients and season to suit yourself.

Note: The more delicious the breadcrumbs (pumpernickel, dill, rye?), the better.

160

HOW TO ASSEMBLE YOUR CHEESE STRUDEL

☆ Melt ¼ pound butter for every two rolls (six servings.)

☆ Have on hand
- a well-greased tray for baking
- a pastry brush
- defrosted strudel leaves, unwrapped, and covered with a slightly damp towel
- the filling
- optional: ¼ cup sesame seeds or wheat germ, to sprinkle on top.

☆ PREHEAT OVEN TO 375°.

Clean off a large, flat working surface. Formica or wood are best.

Place one rectangle of filo down in front of you, so that its length stretches forward in front of you. Brush it generously with melted butter. Place another leaf directly on top of the first, and brush it with more butter. Continue the layering and buttering until you have a pile of four. Butter the top leaf too.

Now:

Apply half your filling (half of one recipe, that is), to the pile, approximately here

Leave at least 1½ inches free at bottom and sides. Fold the sides over, and gently roll the strudel forward.

With all the care you can muster, lift the roll slowly.... use spatulas if you need to....... and place it on the buttered tray.

Repeat this procedure with roll #2, then brush lots of butter onto the completed strudels. Sprinkle with sesame seeds or wheat germ. Slash, with serrated knife, through the top to the filling — 3 or 4 slashes on the diagonal:

Bake 30 minutes, or until golden and crisp.

Polenta Pizza

~ a vegetable & cheese pie
with a cornmeal crust~

1¼ hours
to prepare.

1 9-inch pie.
↳ Preheat oven to 375°F.

(First: Butter a 9-inch pie pan)

CRUST: 1½ cups yellow corn meal   ¼ tsp. salt
        1 cup cold water   ⅓ cup grated parmesan
        1 cup boiling water (heated in a medium saucepan)

1) Place the cornmeal in a small bowl. Add cold water, and stir until uniformly combined.

2) Stir cornmeal mixture into saucepan of boiling water. Cook, stirring, over low heat until thick (about 5 minutes).

3) Remove from heat, and stir in salt and parmesan. Form a crust in the buttered pan. (Use wet hands and/or a spatula to pat it into place.) Bake uncovered for 30 minutes at 375°F. Remove from oven.

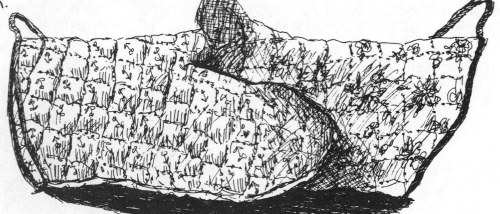

~ Turn oven down to 350°F. ~

FILLING: 1 Tbs. olive oil   ½ tsp. oregano
          1 large clove garlic, crushed   ½ tsp. basil
          ½ cup minced onion   salt, red & black pepper- to taste
          ½ cup sliced bell pepper   ⅓ lb. mozzarella, sliced
          (optional: a few sliced   1 medium tomato, sliced
                mushrooms)   parmesan, for the top

1) Sauté garlic, onion, peppers (and mushrooms) in olive oil for about 5 minutes (until vegetables are tender). Remove from heat; add herbs.

2) Spread sautéed mixture into crust. Arrange slices of mozzarella and tomato on top. Sprinkle generously with parmesan.

Bake 20 minutes at 350°F.

MEXICAN PEPPER CASSEROLE

...spicy sautéed peppers, layered with cheese, topped with a sour cream custard. And it's not difficult to make.

About 1½-2 hours to prepare, including baking time

6 servings
Preheat oven to 375°

6 medium bell peppers
(try to get a mixture
of red and green)

1½ cups thinly-sliced onion

2 Tbs. each – butter and olive oil

3 medium cloves crushed garlic

1 tsp. each: salt
              cumin
              coriander

½ tsp. dry mustard

¼ tsp. each – black and red
                    pepper

2 Tbs. flour

½ lb. medium-
sharp cheddar,
thinly-sliced

paprika

The Custard:

Beat together: { 4 large eggs
                 1½ cups sour cream
                 (you can use
                 part yogurt)

Slice the peppers in thin strips. Heat butter and olive oil together in a heavy skillet. Sauté onions and garlic with salt and spices. When onions are translucent, add peppers. Sauté over low heat for about 10 minutes. Sprinkle in the flour. Mix well and sauté until there is no extra liquid.

Butter a deep casserole. Spread in half the sauté, topped with half the sliced cheese. Repeat these layers. Pour custard over & sprinkle with paprika. Bake 40-45 minutes.   (uncover for last 15 minutes.)

VEGETARIAN SHISH-KEBAB

...Skewered, premarinated vegetable chunks, broiled or barbequed. Serve them on a bed of rice, sprinkled with parmesan cheese.

Plan on two skewers per person. Plan also on giving your eggplant and mushrooms at least 3 hours to marinate.

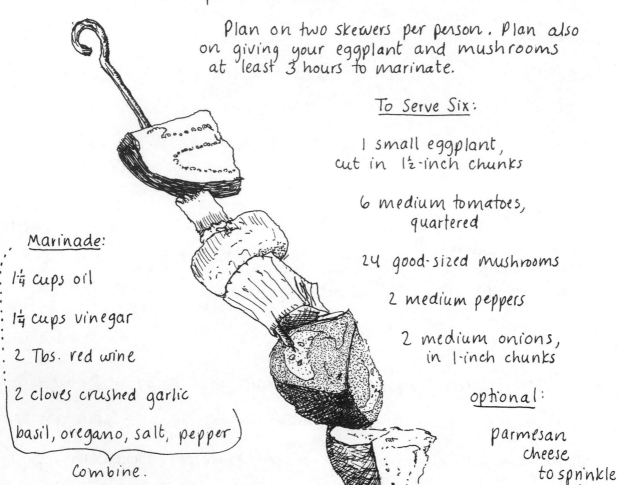

To Serve Six:

1 small eggplant, cut in 1½-inch chunks

6 medium tomatoes, quartered

24 good-sized mushrooms

2 medium peppers

2 medium onions, in 1-inch chunks

optional:

parmesan cheese to sprinkle on top.

Marinade:

1¼ cups oil

1¼ cups vinegar

2 Tbs. red wine

2 cloves crushed garlic

basil, oregano, salt, pepper

Combine.

Clean the mushrooms and marinate them whole. Broil the eggplant chunks until soft (but not mushy) and add them, still hot, to the marinade. Stir and let stand at least 3 hours.

Cut the peppers in wide strips. Skewer the vegetables in a subtle and provocative sequence, and baste them with extra marinade as they barbeque, roast, or broil.

Serve them to your delighted guests, and mention that the skewers might be hot. A good red wine is appropriate with this meal.

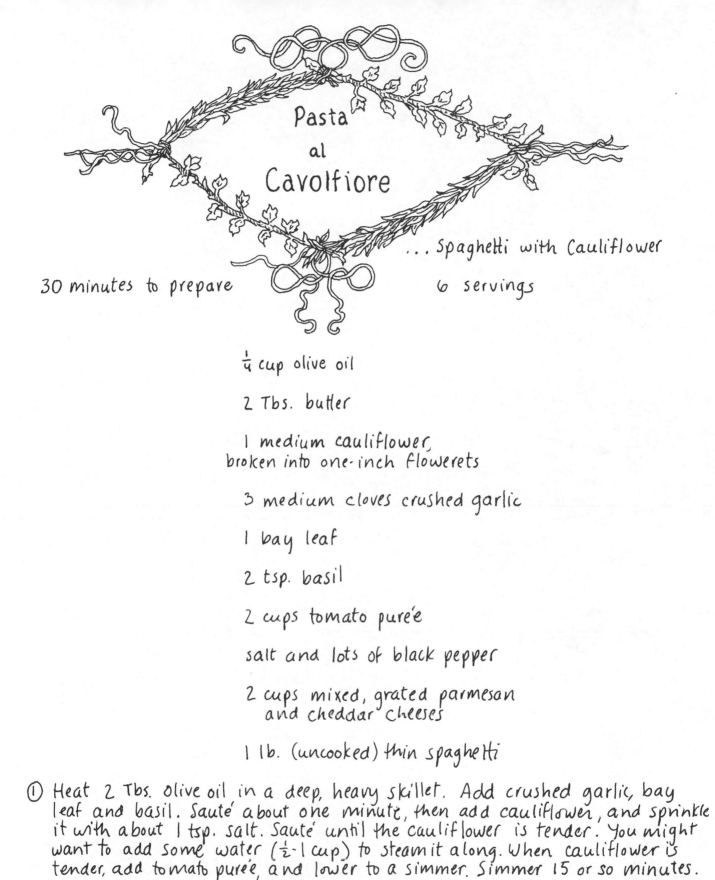

Pasta al Cavolfiore

... Spaghetti with Cauliflower

30 minutes to prepare   6 servings

¼ cup olive oil

2 Tbs. butter

1 medium cauliflower,
broken into one-inch flowerets

3 medium cloves crushed garlic

1 bay leaf

2 tsp. basil

2 cups tomato purée

salt and lots of black pepper

2 cups mixed, grated parmesan
    and cheddar cheeses

1 lb. (uncooked) thin spaghetti

① Heat 2 Tbs. olive oil in a deep, heavy skillet. Add crushed garlic, bay leaf and basil. Sauté about one minute, then add cauliflower, and sprinkle it with about 1 tsp. salt. Sauté until the cauliflower is tender. You might want to add some water (½-1 cup) to steam it along. When cauliflower is tender, add tomato purée, and lower to a simmer. Simmer 15 or so minutes.

② Cook the spaghetti in plenty of boiling water. (8-10 minutes) Drain and toss with remaining olive oil, butter and half the cheese. Spread onto a platter and pour the cauliflower sauce over. Top with more cheese. Serve immediately.

Ricotta Gnocchi
("nyucki")

... Italian Cheese Dumplings

6 servings

Begin these in the morning. They need time to chill.

2 cups (1 lb.) ricotta cheese

2 beaten eggs

½ cup freshly-grated parmesan

⅔ cup (packed) grated mozzarella

(Butter

extra flour

extra parmesan)

black pepper

⅔ cup flour

optional: ¼ cup minced scallion

½ tsp. salt

Optional: ¼ tsp. minced garlic

Combine all ingredients (except butter, extra flour and extra parmesan) and beat well with a fork. Chill two hours.

Flour your hands and make the batter into little balls (about 1-inch in diameter), rolling them until firm between your palms. Roll them in flour; shake off the excess. Place them, single layer, on a tray. Refrigerate another two hours.

Heat a large kettleful of salted water to boiling. Lower to a simmer. Drop the balls in, one-at-a-time, and simmer with a lid on for ten minutes. Remove with a slotted spoon and place on a buttered baking tray. (You probably will have to simmer the gnocchi in shifts - don't try to crowd them in to the kettle.)

Just before serving, broil the balls until golden brown on all sides. Drizzle them with melted butter and sprinkle with grated parmesan as you broil them and turn them. The cheese and butter will make a crisp, delicious coating. Serve over spinach noodles, topped with parsley butter (chopped parsley in melted butter) OR Pesto Sauce (in sauce chapter) for added elegance.

Tomato-Egg Curry

45 minutes
to prepare.

4-5 servings

→ Put your rice on to cook when you begin cooking the curry. (2½ cups raw)
→ Have 3 hardboiled eggs cooked and peeled before-hand.

1½ cups chopped onion
3 cloves garlic
2 tsp. mustard seeds
2 tsp. fresh-grated ginger
½ tsp. salt

Cook in 3 Tbs. butter
in large saucepan
until onion is
translucent.

Then add:

3 cups freshly-diced tomatoes
2 cups tomato purée
1 chopped sweet green pepper
½ tsp. ground cinnamon
1½-2 tsp. ground cumin
½ tsp. ground fenugreek *
½ tsp. ground coriander
½ tsp. salt
¼ tsp. cayenne

Mix well. Cover and simmer over very low heat 15-20 minutes.

Taste to correct salt and other seasonings.

Serve hot, over rice, with wedges of Egg artfully arranged

on top. Pass bowls of yogurt, raisins, toasted almonds or cashews.

* Available at herb shops. It is also used as a tea, so if it's not
with the spices, it might be with the exotic teas.

Eggplant Scallopini

serve
with
dry,
red
wine.

4-6 generous servings

This takes approximately one hour to prepare.

During the last ten minutes of simmering time, prepare your pasta and salad.

4 cups cubed eggplant

1 lb. chopped mushrooms

3 cloves crushed garlic

1 cup (grated) fresh parmesan

1 cup chopped onions

fresh black pepper

1 cup chopped green pepper

1 bay leaf

fresh-chopped parsley (¼ cup)

2 Tbs. olive oil

1 tsp. basil

2 Tbs. butter

1 tsp. salt

2 medium tomatoes, chopped

1 cup Marsala

¼ cup tomato paste

Heat the olive oil and butter in a large, heavy skillet. Add the onions, garlic, ½ tsp. salt, and bay leaf and sauté 5 minutes. Add eggplant and another ½ tsp. salt, stir, and cook, covered, 10 minutes, stirring occasionally. Add mushrooms, remaining salt, spices (not parsley) peppers, tomatoes and paste. Mix well and simmer, covered, 10 minutes. Add marsala and parsley. Cover and simmer over low heat, about 15-20 minutes. Just before serving, mix in the parmesan cheese. Serve over pasta, and pass around some extra parmesan.

Sweet Potato Pancakes

30 minutes to prepare   4-6 servings

1 cup grated carrot
1 cup grated white potato   } firmly-packed

4 beaten eggs   1 packed cup grated
                                        sweet potato

⅓ cup flour   2 Tbs. grated onion

1 tsp. salt   ¼ cup chopped parsley

fresh black pepper   dash of nutmeg

juice of ½ lemon   optional: 1 small
                                        clove crushed
                                        garlic

Place grated sweet and white potatoes in a colander over a bowl. Salt lightly and let stand 15 minutes. Rinse and squeeze out well to get rid of all the extra water (you could save this water for soup stock).

Combine all ingredients and mix well. Fry in butter in a heavy skillet until brown and crisp.

Serve immediately, topped with yogurt or sour cream and fresh-chopped chives. Garnish with tomato wedges and lots of fresh, raw vegetable sticks.

169

⬛ Vegetarian Eggrolls ⬛

These will require a special trip to your local oriental foods shop with the following shopping list:

one pound fresh mung sprouts
a one-pound pack of eggroll skins (usually frozen)
one ounce dried black mushrooms
one small can water chestnuts
a two-inch piece fresh ginger root
a jar of Chinese hot mustard
a jar of Duck or Plum Sauce (or-make your own. Theres a recipe in the sauce chapter.)

Give yourself about a three-hour head-start on this project. There's much chopping involved, and the filling needs to be pre-cooked, cooled and drained before the rolls can be filled and fried.

Your one-pound package of eggroll skins will contain enough for 12-14 large rolls. Two per person are enough for a main dish. If you want to serve the eggrolls as appetizers, cut them into smaller chunks after they're fried. You'll have enough for a good-sized crowd. And you can always freeze a filled, unfried eggroll. Just dust the outside with a little extra corn starch, place on a corn-starched plate, and seal the whole thing in a plastic bag. Don't defrost before frying- just pop the frozen eggrolls into hot oil.

THE FILLING

Have everything chopped and ready before you sauté.

4 cups shredded green cabbage

1½ cups sliced onion

3-4 medium garlic cloves

3 tsp. freshly-grated ginger root

1 lb. fresh mung bean sprouts

2 cups thinly-sliced celery

1 oz. dried black mushroom
(soaked 20 minutes in boiling water; drained and thinly-sliced)

½ cup dry sherry or Chinese rice wine

¼ cup tamari sauce

salt, black pepper

2 minced scallions (include the greens)

½ cup minced green pepper

3 Tbs. safflower, soy or peanut oil

2 tsp. sugar

1 cup thinly-sliced water chestnuts

1 Tbs. sesame seeds

Use a wok or a large cast-iron or stainless-steel skillet. Heat the oil first, and add the crushed garlic and ginger. Toss for several minutes over medium heat, then add the onions and sprinkle lightly with salt. Stir and fry for five minutes before throwing in the cabbage and celery. Salt lightly again, and shake in a generous amount of black pepper.

Stir and fry 8-10 minutes. Add sherry, sugar, mushrooms, water chestnuts, bean sprouts and sesame seeds. Stir-fry over medium-high heat for about 8 more minutes, until the liquid partially evaporates. Remove from heat.

Add raw scallions and green pepper and toss in tamari sauce. Let stand 20-30 minutes, until cool. Drain it by placing a collander or large strainer over a kettle and pouring the filling in. Let it sit and drain at least 15 minutes. (Save the drained-off liquid for soup, sauce or vegetable-steaming water.) Now, taste your filling to correct the seasoning. It may want more salt, pepper or sherry. Hopefully, it won't want less. In any case, pour yourself a glass of sherry and take a break. Sit down and meditate on the shape of Envelopes.

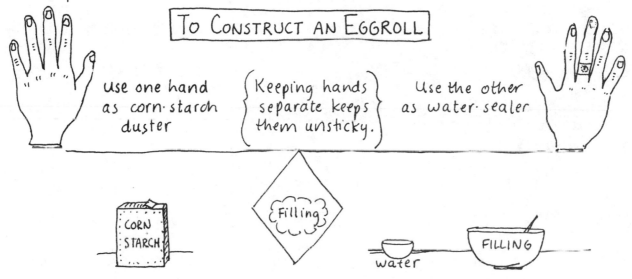

TO CONSTRUCT AN EGGROLL

Use one hand as corn-starch duster

(Keeping hands separate keeps them unsticky.)

Use the other as water-sealer

CORN STARCH

Filling

water

FILLING

① Place a skin down on the surface in front of you on the diamond-axis.

② Lightly dust some corn starch onto surface of same skin.

③ Place a healthy ½-cupful of filling on the lower center section.

④ Roll up as if it were an envelope, folding in the sides, so that no filling is exposed or otherwise threatened.

⑤ Sprinkle some water on the top point and the roll will seal itself.

⑥ Dust the completed roll with cornstarch. Set aside and repeat until all rolls are filled.

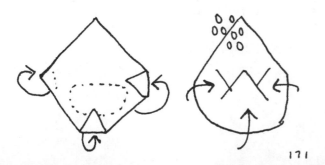

171

continued on next page →

TO FRY AN EGGROLL

Use "all-purpose" vegetable or Planter's peanut oil

Pour enough oil into your wok or skillet to make a pool two to three inches deep. Heat oil on medium-high until it is hot enough to bounce a drop of water immediately upon contact. Be careful to toss only a <u>drop</u> of water in. <u>BE PATIENT</u>. If the oil is not hot enough when you immerse the eggrolls, they'll sponge up all the oil and you will have inedible greaselings.

Fry several rolls at a time - as many as possible without crowding. Keep the heat up fairly high all through the frying. Using a tongs, turn the rolls periodically until they are evenly endowed with crispness, brownness and little airbubbles.

Have ready a pan lined with several thicknesses of paper towels. Drain the eggrolls thoroughly and keep them warm in a 200° oven until you have fried as many as you want for the first round. (Don't stack them up in the pan or they'll get soggy.)

Serve with plenty of hot mustard and duck sauce.

Try them with Tofu Salad (see salad chapter) for a beautiful Eastern meal.

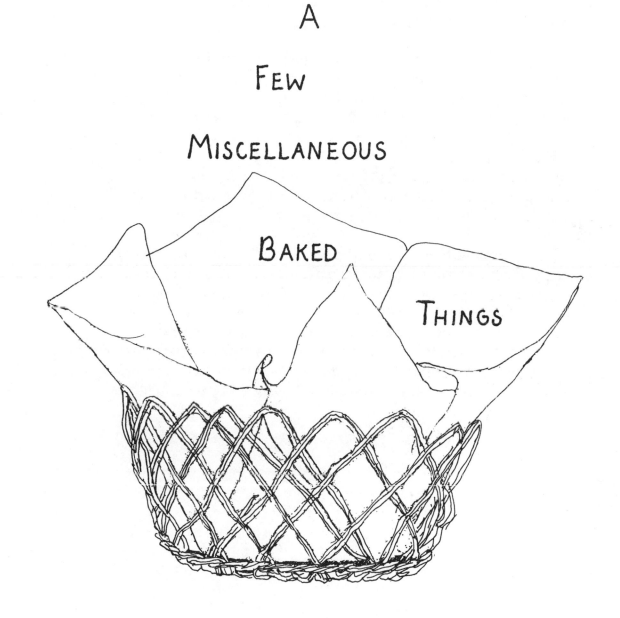

A

FEW

MISCELLANEOUS

BAKED

THINGS

We don't do much bread-baking at Moosewood, because the kitchen is small, and there happens to be a wonderful bakery down the hall from us in the same building. The bakery is called Somadhara, and they bake many varieties of exquisite, whole-grain bread. We serve fresh Somadhara bread at Moosewood.

We do prepare corn breads, though, and two corn bread recipes appear in this section.

Pita (pocket bread) and tortillas are frequent components of Moosewood fare, and although it is too great a task for us to bake the necessary quantities of these at the restaurant (we usually buy pita and tortillas in bulk), I have included recipes for them here. Since many of the folks using this book are preparing home-sized amounts of food, it is feasible to bake your own pita and tortillas. So here is the information, providing you with the choice of baking or buying.

Two other items are presented here: an original recipe for homemade crackers and a recipe for custardy popovers. The crackers are here to provide you with a special companion for the many spread and dip recipes in this book. The popovers are easy and wonderful. I find myself serving them frequently as an accompaniment to Moosewood soups and salads made at home. They add elegance to any meal. They can also be a whole breakfast, in and of themselves.

Homemade Sesame Crackers

1 cup whole wheat flour

1 cup white flour

1 tsp. salt

1½ tsp. baking powder

2 Tbs. sesame seeds

1 Tbs. butter

¼ cup yogurt

scant ⅔ cup ice water

① Preheat oven to 350°.

② Sift together the first four ingredients twice.

③ Cut in the yogurt.

④ Melt the butter in a little tiny pan. Toast the sesame seeds in the butter until they are perfect.

⑤ Add toasted sesame seeds to batter.

⑥ Mix in the ice water. Knead lightly (20 strokes).

⑦ Roll to ⅛-inch thick. Cut with knife or cooky cutter. Prick all over with a fork.

⑧ Bake on a lightly-greased cooky sheet 10 minutes, or until lightly brown. Cool them on a rack. They will crispen as they cool.

Variation: Rye flour & caraway seeds instead of whole wheat and sesame.

175

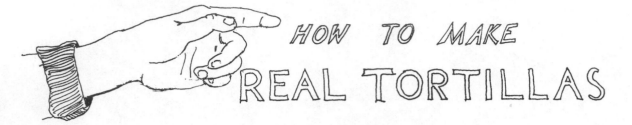

HOW TO MAKE
REAL TORTILLAS

There are only two ingredients necessary for making authentic tortillas at home. One is water. The other is something you may never have heard of: Masa Harina. It might sound like the name of a Mexican night club entertainer, but masa harina is actually a special kind of corn meal. It is ground in a special way and treated with lime water. Its flavor is induplicable - don't substitute anything else in this recipe, expecting to emerge with Real Tortillas. Regular corn meal won't do it.

So where does one find masa Harina? Every third or forth supermarket seems to have it. It is usually stored near cereals and flours and corn meals. Shop around for it. These tortillas are so easy to make and so wonderful to eat, they are worth the trouble of tracking down some full-fledged masa harina.

<u>For Twelve Delectable Tortillas</u>:

2 cups masa harina   1¼ cups water (approximately)
              optional: dash of salt

Mix masa harina and water together (and salt, if you choose), first with a fork, and eventually with your hands. Knead for about five minutes. You may have to add a little extra water. The dough should hold together. Make 12 equal balls - smooth and round. Roll each ball on one side only, on an unfloured surface (formica works well) or between 2 sheets of waxed paper, to ⅛" thick. Trim the edges of the circle with a knife. You should emerge with a neat, clean, thin 6-inch round.   Pan-fry on a lightly-greased griddle or heavy skillet over medium heat, 3-4 minutes on each side. Wrap in a damp towel, and keep them warm in a 200° oven until serving time.

CUSTARDY POPOVERS

15 minutes to prepare
35 minutes to bake

12 popovers
375° oven

~crisp and puffy, full of hot air, with a layer
of custard on the inside.

4 eggs

1 cup unbleached
white flour

1 cup milk

$\frac{1}{2}$ tsp. salt

4 Tbs. melted butter

① Beat together the eggs and milk. Add flour and salt. Beat with a fork until mixture is uniform.
② Preheat the muffin tin in the oven 5 minutes. Brush the cups and the top surface generously with melted butter.
③ Fill each muffin hole 2/3-full with batter. Work quickly so the tin stays hot. Place in the oven.
④ Bake for 35 minutes without opening the oven. Prick each popover with a fork, to let steam escape. (This will help them hold their shape.) Serve immediately, with butter and jam.

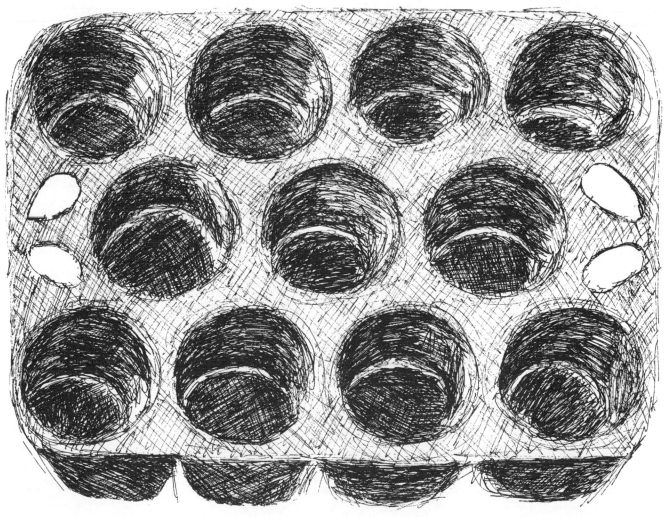

DELICIOUS CORN BREAD

20 minutes to bake

one 8-inch pan

425° oven

¼ cup honey

1 cup buttermilk

1 egg

1 cup yellow corn meal

1 cup unbleached white flour

2 tsp. baking powder

½ tsp. baking soda

½ tsp. salt

3 Tbs. melted butter

1- Beat together egg, buttermilk and honey.

2- Mix well together all dry ingredients.

3- Combine all ingredients, including melted butter, and mix well.

4- Spread into buttered 8-inch square pan, and bake.

Serve hot with butter and a chunk of cheddar cheese.

Serve with Pepper & Onion Shortcake, Spicy Pepper Sandwich (in "Grilled Vegetable Sandwiches), Vegetarian Chili, Cheese-Beans or for breakfast.

Mexican Corn & Cheese Bread

25-30 minutes to bake   one 8-inch square pan

375° oven

1 cup unbleached white flour

1 cup yellow corn meal

1 egg, lightly-beaten

2 Tbs. honey

3 tsp. baking powder

$\frac{1}{2}$ tsp. salt

1 cup milk

$\frac{1}{4}$ cup olive oil

$\frac{1}{2}$ cup finely-minced onion

1 cup fresh or frozen corn (whole kernels)

$\frac{1}{2}$ cup grated cheddar cheese

1- Heat olive oil in a small skillet. Add minced onion, and saute over medium heat 5-8 minutes, or until onion is soft and translucent. Set aside to cool.

2- Beat together egg, honey and milk.

3- Combine thoroughly together flour, corn meal, baking powder, and salt.

4- Combine milk mixture and cornmeal mixture. Mix until well-blended.

5- Add corn kernels, sautéed onions (be sure to scrape in all the excess olive oil from the pan!) and grated cheese. Mix well.

6- Spread into well-buttered 8-inch square pan. Bake at 375° 25-30 minutes, or until brown and firm on top.

Pita Bread
(Arabic Pocket Bread)

About 3 hours
to prepare.

6 large rounds
Each round can be
cut in half to make
two sandwiches.

1½ tsp. active dry yeast

1 cup wrist-temperature water

1 Tbs. honey

1½ tsp. salt

(a little oil)

3 cups flour
(you can use up to half whole wheat)

① Dissolve the yeast in the water with 1 tsp. honey. Let stand five minutes.

② Add remaining honey, flour and salt, mixing enthusiastically with a wooden spoon until well-combined.

③ Turn out and knead 10 minutes. Add a little more flour if it's sticky.

④ Oil the mixing bowl, return the dough to it, and lightly oil the top surface of the dough. Cover and let rise 1½ hours in a warm place.

⑤ Punch the dough down and knead again for a few minutes. Divide it into six equal parts. Form each part into a smooth, round ball. Cover the balls with a clean towel and let stand fifteen minutes.

→ LIGHT THE OVEN TO 475° WHEN YOU SET THE BALLS OUT TO STAND. THE OVEN MUST BE FULLY-PREHEATED FOR BAKING, AS THE HIGH TEMPERATURE IS THE MAGIC POCKETING FACTOR!

⑥ Roll each ball to ½-inch thickness. Place on an ungreased tray. Bake them on the lowest possible oven rack for ten minutes, or until they are puffed-up and turning brown.

⑦ Wrap the freshly-baked breads in a towel and place them in a brown paper bag for 15 minutes. This serves to maintain their pockets as they deflate, preventing them from crispening into crackers.

DESSERTS

Desserts needn't always be decadent, indulgent experiences. (Only sometimes.) At Moosewood we try to have healthful (ie-Whole-wheated, honey or maple syrup-sweetened, freshly-fruited) dessert choices in addition to our homemade, honey-sweetened ice cream, and complementary to our immodestly-rich chocolate fudge brownies (reverenced by hedonists) and occasional other excessive treats.

The idea is to present people with a choice which acknowl-edges the fact that we are all human beings whose sensuality and sensibility take turns dictating tastes harmoniously as possible. Variety without too huge a dose of dogma is a goal.

Some of these desserts are high in protein and comprehensive enough for brunch or High Tea or other aesthetic rituals. These items include Fruited Yogurt Desserts, Maple Egg Custard, Apple-Honey Custard Pie, Creamy Rice Pudding, Ricotta Cake, Bread Pudding, Finnish Whipped Fruit Puddings and the two strudels. The Fruited Yogurt and Ricotta Cake, in particular are not only high in protein, but also generously low-in-fat.

If you prefer not to use sugar, almost all these desserts can be sweetened with honey or maple syrup (and many of them are anyway). The only exceptions are Date Nut Torte, SourCream-Orange Cake, Ukrainian Poppyseed Cake, Fudge Brownies (not to be confused with Carob Brownies), Pound Cake and its Variations, and Cardamom Coffee Cake.

Date - Nut Torte

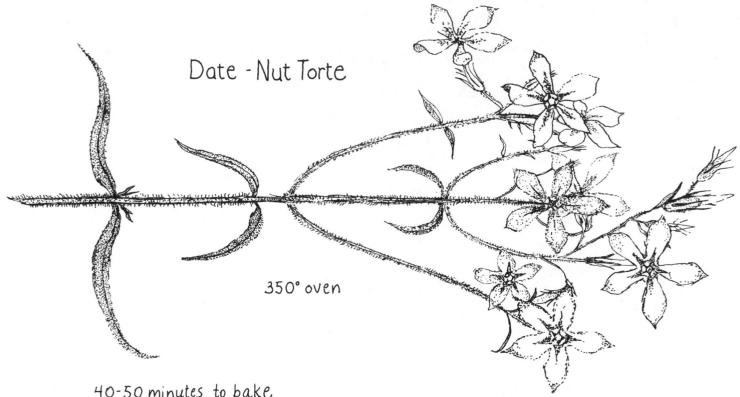

350° oven

40-50 minutes to bake

1 9-inch round (buttered & floured)

⅓ cup flour	3 separated eggs
1 tsp. baking powder	½ cup brown sugar
¼ tsp. salt	½ tsp. vanilla
¾ cup finely-chopped nuts	1 cup chopped dates

½ pint heavy cream } whipped,
¼ tsp. vanilla } for the top

① Beat egg whites, with salt, until stiff.

② Beat egg yolks with sugar until thick. Add vanilla and mix.

③ Add dry ingredients. Blend well. Mix in the dates.

④ Fold egg whites into batter. Pour into pan and bake.

⑤ When cool, turn upside-down on a serving plate. The center of the torte will fall slightly, leaving a little ridge-around-the edge. Fill the top with lots of whipped cream.

Yogurt-Cream Cheese Pie

crust-topping:

    2 cups crushed graham crackers
    ¼ cup butter, melted w/. 2 Tbs. honey
    ½ tsp. cinnamon
    dash nutmeg
    (optional: ½ cup very finely-chopped (not ground) & toasted nuts
          OR- 2 Tbs. toasted sesame seeds)

Press mixture firmly into sides & bottom of an 8" pie pan.
Reserve extra crumbs for topping.

filling:

    8 oz. softened cream cheese
    ½ cup firm yogurt
    ¼ cup honey
    1½ tsp. pure vanilla
    grated rind of ½ lemon (or 1 lime or ⅓ orange)

Beat w/ electric mixer till well-blended. Spread into shell,
top w/ crumbs.

Chill at least 3 hours

Sour Cream - Orange Cake

Baking Time:
50-60 minutes.

Preheat oven to 350°F.

Butter a tube or bundt pan.

1½ cups (3 sticks) softened butter
1¾ cups sugar
4 large eggs (at room temperature)
½ tsp. each: lemon & orange rind
½ tsp. vanilla extract
3 cups unbleached white flour
3 tsp. baking powder
1 tsp. baking soda
½ tsp. salt
1½ cups sour cream (→ Yogurt may
be substituted!)

OPTIONAL SYRUP:
¼ cup orange juice (fresh-squeezed, if possible)
3 Tbs. orange liqueur
2 Tbs. sugar
1 Tbs. lemon juice

1) In a large mixing bowl, cream together the butter and sugar.
2) Add the eggs, one at a time, beating well after each.
3) Stir in citrus rinds and vanilla. Set aside.
4) In a separate bowl sift together the flour, powder, soda, and salt.
5) Add the dry ingredient mixture to the butter mixture alternately with the sour cream or yogurt. Stir well after each addition (but don't beat).
6) Turn into prepared pan. Bake 50-60 minutes, and/or until springy to the touch, and/or until a cake tester comes out clean.
7) Cool, then invert onto a plate with a rim. (The cake is delicious just as is, but even moreso with the syrup.)
8) To make the syrup, heat the ingredients together in a small saucepan - to boiling. Cook over medium heat 2-3 minutes.
9) Pour hot syrup over cooled cake. Let stand at least 10 minutes before slicing.

Apple Krisp

6-8 servings

8-10 medium
cooking apples

juice of 1 lemon

2 cups raw oats

¼ cup walnuts

¼ cup sunflower seeds

½ cup orange juice

¾ cup flour

½ cup butter

⅓ cup honey

1 tsp. cinnamon

½ tsp. allspice

½ tsp. salt

Peel (if necessary), pare and slice the apples. Drizzle them with fresh lemon juice. Spread half of them into a large, oblong pan.

Melt the butter and honey together. Combine with oats, flour, nuts, seeds, salt and spices. Spread ½ this mixture (actually <u>crumble</u>, it won't really spread) onto apples in pan. Cover with the remaining apples and the rest of the topping. Pour O. J. over the top. Bake 40-45 minutes, uncovered, at 375°. Cover if it crisps too quickly.

<u>Notes</u>: ① If you'd be uncomfortable leaving raisins out, you are allowed to add some. Put them in with the apples so they won't burn.

② Throw in some cranberries for a jeweled effect.

③ Substitute pears or peaches for the apples
reduce baking time to 25 minutes.

186

Montana's Mom's Dynamite Cheesecake

"loved by millions from coast to coast" ~ montana

oven 375°

CRUST: crumbs from 16 graham crackers
½ stick butter
1 Tbs. honey
1 Tbs. flour
~mush up w/ fingers and press firmly into bottom
of spring-form pan.

FILLING: 16 oz. cream cheese
⅓ c. sugar
4 eggs
1 tsp. vanilla
1 lemon: juice and grated rind
~blend till smooth and creamy. Pour on top of crust
and bake for 25 minutes –or until set at 375°.

COOL.

TOPPING: 1 pt. sour cream
½ cup sugar
1 tsp. vanilla
~blend. Pour on top of cooled filling and bake
at 375° for 5-8 minutes.

A MUST: cheesecake must set in refrigerator for <u>at least</u>
12 hours before it will be firm enough to slice well.
If you get impatient and cut before it is completely
set, the top will be runny.

Carrot Cake

350° oven
40-50 minutes to bake

2 loaves

1½ cups melted butter
1¾ cups brown sugar
(OR 1½ cups honey)
4 eggs, room temperature
3 tsp. vanilla extract
Grated rind of 1 lemon

} Beat in large bowl, beginning with sugar or honey and butter, add eggs one-at-a-time. Add remaining ingredients, and beat until light in color.

2 cups whole wheat flour
2 cups white flour
1 tsp. salt
½ tsp. baking soda
3 tsp. baking powder
1 tsp. ground allspice
2 tsp. ground cinnamon

} Sift together twice.

2½ cups, packed, finely shredded carrot, soaked in juice of 1 lemon.

Optional: ¾ cup each currants or nuts

Add flour mixture and grated carrot alternately to butter mixture, beginning and ending with flour (flour - carrot - flour - carrot - flour). After each addition mix gently to combine, but do not beat or otherwise overmix - this toughens and dries a cake. Add nuts and raisins last. Generously butter 2 loaf pans and sprinkle with poppy seeds (they'll stick to the butter.)

Divide batter and bake.

Cool 10 minutes in the pan, then remove to finish cooling.

Serve plain, or with butter or cream cheese.

Banana Bread

~Basically the same method as Carrot Cake,
but with the following changes:

1) Use <u>one cup</u> (2 sticks) butter — softened, not melted

2) Use 1⅓ cups (packed) brown sugar (not honey)

3) <u>3</u> eggs

4) 2 tsp. vanilla plus ¼ tsp. almond extract

5) 1 tsp. grated orange rind (instead of lemon)

6) Substitute ¼ tsp. nutmeg for allspice.

7) Replace carrot with:
   1½ cups mashed ripe banana } puréed together
   <u>plus</u> ⅔ cup black coffee

8) Replace poppyseeds with sesame seeds.

189

Ukrainian Poppyseed Cake

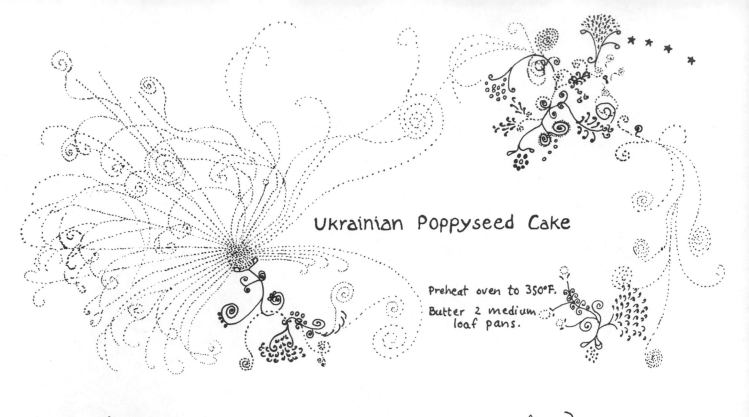

Preheat oven to 350°F.

Butter 2 medium loaf pans.

¾ cup poppyseeds	2 cups unbleached white flour ⎫
1 cup milk	3 tsp. baking powder ⎬ sifted together
½ lb. (2 sticks) butter	½ tsp. salt ⎭
1⅓ cups light brown sugar	½ tsp. vanilla
3 eggs	1 tsp. lemon rind

1) Heat poppyseeds and milk together in a saucepan. Remove from heat right before it boils. Let stand until room temperature.

2) Cream butter with sugar. Add eggs, one at a time, beating <u>well</u> after each.

3) Add sifted dry ingredients alternately with poppyseed mixture, stirring well after each addition. Stir in vanilla and lemon rind at the end.

4) Bake in well-greased loaf pans at 350°F for 40-50 minutes, or until cake-tester comes out clean.

Fruited Yogurt Desserts

Combine
all ingredients
gently.

Serve chilled.

Each of these
serves six.

I.

3 cups plain yogurt

1 cup fresh blueberries

1 cup fresh, pitted cherries

maple syrup or honey to taste

$\frac{1}{2}$ tsp. pure vanilla extract

II.

3 cups plain yogurt

$1\frac{1}{2}$ cups fresh peach slices

1 cup fresh strawberries
(halved)

honey to taste

1 mashed, ripe banana

$\frac{1}{2}$ tsp. pure vanilla extract

III.

3 cups plain yogurt

3 cups grated apples

$\frac{1}{2}$ cup chopped, toasted almonds

$\frac{1}{2}$ cup maple syrup

dash each of cinnamon & nutmeg

(optional: $\frac{1}{4}$ cups raisins or
toasted sunflower seeds)

191

... Moosewood Fudge Brownies ...

let soften: ½ lb. butter (don't melt it)

Melt: 5 oz. unsweetened chocolate. Let cool.
  (& make sure it's bitter & not semisweet)

Cream the butter with 1¾ cups (packed) light brown sugar and 5 eggs. Add 1½ tsp. pure vanilla extract. Beat in the melted, cooled chocolate and 1 cup flour.

Spread into a buttered 9 x 13" baking pan. Bake 20-30 minutes at 350°.

Optional: chopped nuts -OR-

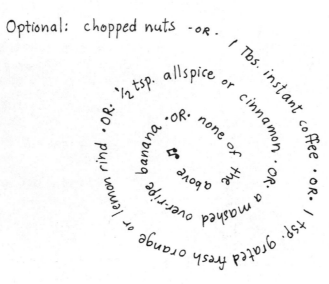

1 Tbs. instant coffee ·OR· ½ tsp. allspice or cinnamon ·OR· a mashed over-ripe banana ·OR· 1 tsp. grated fresh orange or lemon rind ·OR· none of the above

Yet another option: instead of uniformly blending in the chocolate, you can marble it. Add chocolate last, after the flour is completely blended in and only partially blend in the chocolate. It looks real nice

Creamy Rice Pudding

350° oven
Butter an 8" square pan.

25 minutes,
baking time

2 cups cooked rice (1 cup raw,
cooked slowly in 2 cups water
until well-done)

optional:

1 cup grated apple
1 cup fresh peach
            slices
½ cup chopped nuts

mix in with
the rice

2 eggs
1 cup milk
⅓ cup honey
1 tsp. vanilla
½ tsp. salt
handful of raisins or chopped
                        dates

½ tsp. cinnamon
dash or 2 of nutmeg
2 tsp. fresh lemon juice

1 cup of one of → yogurt
                → sour cream
                → whipped cream

Beat eggs, milk and honey together in a blender. Combine with cooked rice and remaining ingredients, except yogurt, sour cream or heavy cream. Spread into a buttered 8" square pan (or its equivalent) and bake. Stir well every 8-10 minutes during baking. Remove from oven after 25 minutes. It'll still be loose, but will solidify as it cools.

After it has cooled 10 minutes, stir in the yogurt, sour or heavy cream. Eat it hot, warm or cold.

Apple~Honey
Custard
Pie

~easy,
        and wonderful

375° oven   45 minutes, baking time

1 9" pie shell, unbaked

2 cups peeled & sliced apples
   (any kind but red delicious)

4 large eggs

¾ cup honey

optional: Replace apples with sliced, fresh peaches or pitted, halved fresh black cherries

1 cup yogurt

1 tsp. vanilla

optional: a handful of chopped nuts for the top. ...Replace honey with maple syrup

½ tsp. cinnamon

¼ tsp. salt

Spread apple slices evenly over pie shell. Combine remaining
ingredients in the blender, and run at high speed for several seconds.
Pour custard over apples. Sprinkle on some nuts (walnuts or almonds
recommended), if desired. Bake 45 minutes, or until solid when
jiggled. Cool at least to room temperature before cutting.

No-Fault Pumpkin Pie

3 cups pumpkin purée
¾ cup honey
2 Tbs. molasses
¼ tsp. powdered cloves
3 tsp. cinnamon
1½ tsp. ginger
1 tsp. salt
4 eggs, slightly beaten
1 can evaporated milk (or 2 cups scalded milk)

Mix in order given.

Pour into whole wheat pie shell and bake
      10 minutes at 450°, then
      40 minutes at 350°, or till set.

Variation: for a delicious pumpkin pudding, omit pie shell.
      Bake filling in buttered baking dish and serve
      w/ vanilla ice cream or heavy cream.

Apricot-Almond Bread

1 large loaf

350° oven
1¼ hours, baking time

1½ cups dried apricots

1½ cups water

2 Tbs. soft butter

½ cup honey or real maple syrup

1 tsp. salt

1½ cups white flour

1 cup whole wheat flour

1 tsp. soda

2 tsp. baking powder

1 cup chopped almonds

1 beaten egg

1 tsp. vanilla

½ tsp. grated fresh orange rind

Cook apricots in water for 10 minutes (covered, low heat.). Cool completely and add butter, syrup and salt. Beat in egg and vanilla. Sift together dry ingredients. Fold everything together and spread into buttered loaf pan. Bake, and remove bread from pan 10 minutes after it comes out of the oven.

Baked Maple Egg Custard

6 custard cups

350° oven

40-50 minutes,
baking time

4 eggs

dash of cinnamon

⅓ cup real maple syrup

dash of nutmeg

½ tsp. salt

1 tsp. vanilla

2½ cups milk

1½ cups fresh peach slices
(optional)

Beat eggs, slowly adding other ingredients (except peaches). You can use either a wire whisk, an electric mixer or a blender.

Pour into oven-proof custard cups. Place the cups in a deep baking pan. Fill the pan with hot water, almost to the level of the custard. Bake. (Add the peach slices after 20 minutes). When you remove the pan from the oven, remove the cups from the pan, otherwise the custard will continue to cook. Cool to room temperature, then chill thoroughly.

For glazed custard: Cook ½ cup honey in a saucepan until it turns dark. Ladle a little hot honey into each cup so that it coats the bottom. Pour in custard and bake as directed. Before serving loosen edges with a knife and turn custard out, upside-down.

Ricotta Cake

~ Italian-style Cheesecake

-Butter a 10-inch spring-form pan.
-Dust it with flour, fine crumbs, or ground almonds.

Preheat oven to 375°F.

4 large eggs, separated
2 lbs. (4 cups) ricotta cheese
$\frac{3}{4}$ cup sugar
$\frac{1}{3}$ cup unbleached white flour
1 tsp. vanilla extract
$\frac{1}{4}$ tsp. almond extract
dash of salt
$\frac{1}{2}$ tsp. each: orange & lemon rind

(1) Beat egg whites until stiff.

(2) Without cleaning beaters, beat together (in a separate, large bowl) ricotta, egg yolks, sugar, and flour. Beat well.

(3) Stir in extracts, salt, and citrus rinds.

(4) Gently fold in the beaten egg whites. Transfer to the spring-form pan.

(5) Bake 50 minutes at 375°F. Then turn oven off, open the oven door, and leave the cake in there another 15 minutes. Cool completely before serving. (Best if served chilled.)

198

Maple-Walnut Pie

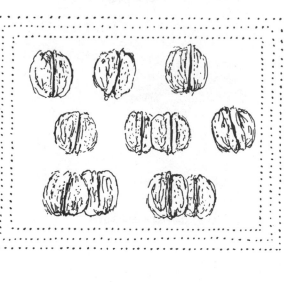

Preparation time
(not including
crust-making):
45 minutes
(including baking)

→ Begin pastry for
crust several hours
earlier. You can use
your own favorite
recipe – or the one
for "Spinach-Ricotta Pie"
p. 123.

Preheat oven
to 375°.

1 unbaked 9" pie shell

4 large eggs

3/4 cup real maple syrup

a few squirts fresh lemon juice

dash of cinnamon

1/4 cup melted butter

1/2 tsp. vanilla

1/2 tsp. salt

2 cups walnut pieces

Beat together everything except walnuts. You can use a blender, wire whisk or electric mixer. Just make sure the mixture is light and smooth.

Spread the walnuts into the unbaked crust. Pour the batter over the nuts and bake 30 minutes, or until solid. Serve warm or cold, with whipped cream or ice cream.

Pound Cake

one full-sized bundt
or tube pan

1 pound sweet butter

3 cups white sugar

6 eggs

1 cup milk

2 tsp. pure vanilla extract

1 Tbs. baking powder

4 cups unbleached white flour

These should
be at
room
temperature.

If you use <u>sweet</u>
butter add ½ tsp.
salt. If you use
regular butter, add
only a dash of salt.

Cream together butter and sugar with an electric mixer
at high speed, until light and fluffy. Add eggs, one-at-a-time, beating
well after each. Remove from electric mixer.

Sift together dry ingredients. Mix together milk and vanilla
extract. Add dry and wet to butter mixture alternately, beginning and
ending with dry. Mix by hand, using a rubber spatula or wooden spoon,
after each addition. Mix thoroughly just enough to blend, without excess
beating.

Pour into buttered & floured bundt or tube pan. Bake 1 hour,
or until toothpick inserted into center comes out dry. After the cake cools
ten minutes, turn it out onto a plate. Let it cool completely before
you slice it.

Poundcake Variations

Here are some delightful adulterations you can perform in your own kitchen.

For each of these variations, follow the Poundcake recipe on the opposite page, with the following changes:

for

Lemon Poundcake
⋮

① Replace vanilla with lemon extract.

② Add the fresh, grated rind of one entire lemon.

for

Blueberry-Lemon Poundcake
⋮

① Replace vanilla with lemon extract.

② At the last stage of folding in dry ingredients, fold in 2 cups fresh blueberries.

③ Add 1tsp. fresh lemon rind.

for

Mocha Swirl Poundcake
⋮

① Replace the milk with one cup strong, black coffee. (double-strength.)

② After batter is all combined, remove ⅓ the batter and mix thoroughly with one ounce-square of melted unsweetened chocolate.

③ Spread non-chocolate batter into tube or bundt pan and spoon clumps of chocolate batter on top. Using a humble dinner knife, swirl the dark and light together with a gentle folding motion - until they mingle in perfect marbled form. Bake as directed.

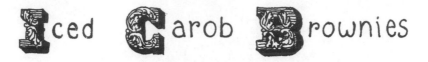 Iced Carob Brownies

Carob is carob. Chocolate is chocolate. For chocolate lovers, there is nothing to take the place of chocolate. But many people expect carob, because of remote similarities, to ring their Chocolate Chimes. That is unfair. Let carob be itself – its genuine, sweet, subtle self. You will discover it to have a charm and character of its own.

½ cup melted butter

¼ cup carob powder
(available in Natural Foods Stores)

2 beaten eggs

½ cup real maple syrup or honey
(or, 1 cup brown sugar)

1 tsp. vanilla extract

1 cup unbleached white flour
(or, ½ white and ½ whole wheat pastry flour)

1 tsp. baking powder

¼ tsp. salt

½ cup raisins

½ cup broken nut meats

Whisk butter and carob together until free of lumps. Add eggs, syrup, honey or sugar, and vanilla.

Stir dry ingredients together, add and mix. Add raisins and walnuts and mix. Pour into buttered 8" square pan and bake 20-25 minutes. Cool before frosting.

 Icing #1

Beat until smooth.
{ ¼ cup soft butter
1 egg
¼ cup carob powder

Add:
½ tsp. instant coffee powder
½ tsp. vanilla
dash of salt
1½ cups powdered sugar

Slowly add: 2 Tbs. heavy cream.
Beat until creamy.

 Icing #2

1) ¼ cup carob powder

2) 8 oz. soft cream cheese

3) ½ tsp. instant coffee powder

4) ¼ cup real maple syrup

5) ½ tsp. vanilla

Beat together 1, 2 and 3.
Add 4 and 5.

Banana-Sour Cream Pie

- 45 minutes to prepare -

- at least 3-4 hours to chill -

one 9-inch pie

NO BAKING!

~ a very, very rich and creamy filling in a graham-cracker-nut crust. The filling contains no eggs.

The Crust:

⅓ lb. (1 "stay-fresh" pkg.) crushed graham crackers

6 Tbs. melted butter

½ tsp. cinnamon   dash of nutmeg

½ cup finely chopped
almonds

Combine all ingredients and mix well. Press firmly into a 9" pie pan, building up thick sides with a nice edge.

The Filling:

12 oz. softened cream cheese
½ cup (packed) light brown sugar

¾ cup mashed, ripe banana   2 Tbs. fresh lemon or lime juice
½ tsp. vanilla extract   ¼ tsp. almond extract
¼ cup sour cream

Beat together
all ingredients
until well-blended.

Pour into crust;
chill 3-4 hours, at least.
(overnight chilling = ideal)

Ginger-Brandy Cheesecake

350° oven   40-50 minutes, baking time

I. CRUST:
    2 cups finely-crumbled ginger snaps
    5 Tbs. butter
    2 Tbs. honey

Melt butter and honey together. Add to snap crumbs and mix well. Press firmly into the floor of an assembled spring-form pan.

II. FILLING:
    12 oz. softened cream cheese
    1 ½ cups sour cream
    4 large eggs
    5 Tbs. honey
    1-2 Tbs. good brandy
    1 tsp. freshly-grated ginger root
    dash of salt

Whip everything together in a high-speed blender until fluffy. Pour into spring-form pan and bake with a pan of water in the oven. The cake is done when a toothpick probing the center emerges with nothing clinging (40-50 minutes).

III. GLAZE: (Wait until cake is completely cool.)

    3/4 cup orange juice
    2 Tbs. corn starch
    2 Tbs. honey
    2 tsp. brandy
    ¼ tsp. orange rind.

Place cornstarch in a small saucepan. Whisk orange juice into it. Cook, whisking constantly, until thick and glossy (approximately 8 minutes.) Remove from heat. Keep whisking and add remaining ingredients. Pour over cooled cheesecake. Decorate with strips of candied ginger, if desired. Chill thoroughly for several hours.

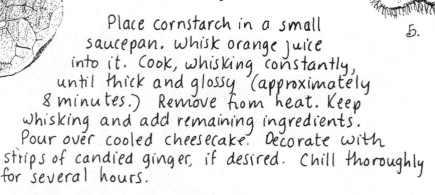

Wild Ginger.

Old-Fashioned
Bread Pudding

350° oven
9x13" pan

This is good for using up old bread, or dried-out cake. You can use leftover banana bread, corn bread (plain, not the onion+cheese kind!), carrot cake, gingerbread — whatever lends itself to your taste.

This recipe is geared for regular, unsweet bread. If you do use cake or a sweet bread, adjust the amounts of sweetening, spice, and vanilla to taste.

· ·

<u>Beat well together:</u>   (you can use a blender)

3 cups milk

3 eggs (large)

$\frac{1}{2}$ tsp. cinnamon $\frac{1}{2}$ tsp. salt   3 Tbs. honey

juice from $\frac{1}{2}$ lemon   2 tsp. vanilla extract   2 Tbs. brown sugar

<u>Mix together in a 9 x 13" baking pan:</u>

4 cups coarsely crumbled
bread

$1\frac{1}{2}$ cups freshly-grated apple $\frac{and}{or}$ $\frac{1}{2}$ cup chopped, dried fruit

$\frac{1}{2}$ cup chopped nuts (optional)

Pour the first mixture into the pan, and push everything around with a wooden spoon until it is uniformly combined.

Bake 35 minutes. Serve hot, warm, or cold with heavy cream ·········or ice cream ······· or fresh fruit ········· or applesauce ·····

205

Cranapple-Walnut Cake

~ very moist ♥♥♥

one 9×13" cake

350° oven
45-50 minutes to bake

You can make this cake with brown sugar or with honey.

1¾ cups light brown sugar
OR
1 cup honey plus 2 Tbs. orange juice
concentrate

½ cup vegetable oil

2 cups flour (you can use ½ whole wheat
pastry flour)

1 tsp. baking soda

1 tsp. cinnamon

½ tsp. nutmeg

1 tsp. salt

2 eggs

1 tsp. vanilla

2 cups sliced cooking apples

½ cup walnut pieces

½ lb. fresh, whole, raw cranberries

(If you use honey, whip it first at high speed, for about 10 minutes or until it turns white and opaque.) Cream together oil and sugar (or, whipped honey plus orange juice concentrate.) Add eggs and vanilla, and beat well. Sift together the flour and dry ingredients. Add to the first mixture and stir until thoroughly combined. Stir in apples, cranberries and nuts.

Bake in a well-greased 9×13" pan, 45-50 minutes at 350°.

Cardamom Coffee Cake

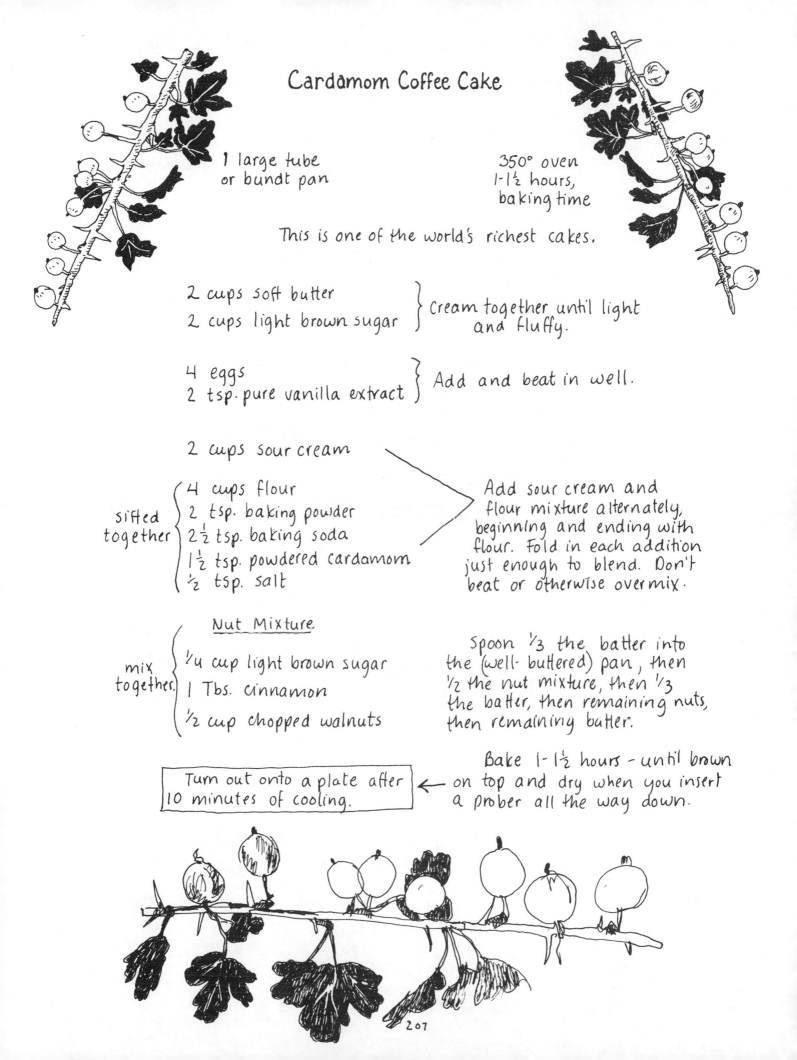

1 large tube
or bundt pan

350° oven
1-1½ hours,
baking time

This is one of the world's richest cakes.

2 cups soft butter
2 cups light brown sugar } Cream together until light and fluffy.

4 eggs
2 tsp. pure vanilla extract } Add and beat in well.

2 cups sour cream

sifted together {
4 cups flour
2 tsp. baking powder
2½ tsp. baking soda
1½ tsp. powdered cardamom
½ tsp. salt

Add sour cream and flour mixture alternately, beginning and ending with flour. Fold in each addition just enough to blend. Don't beat or otherwise overmix.

Nut Mixture

mix together. {
¼ cup light brown sugar
1 Tbs. cinnamon
½ cup chopped walnuts

Spoon ⅓ the batter into the (well-buttered) pan, then ½ the nut mixture, then ⅓ the batter, then remaining nuts, then remaining batter.

Bake 1-1½ hours - until brown on top and dry when you insert a prober all the way down.

Turn out onto a plate after 10 minutes of cooling. ←

Finnish Whipped Fruit Puddings

Mix and match your favorite fruit juices and fruit.

5-6 servings

40 minutes, actual preparation time, but then it needs at least 1½ hours to chill.

3 cups fruit juice (apple, cranberry, orange, pineapple, grape—any or several.) (but NOT Hawaiian Punch.)

½ cup raw farina (non-instant)

½ cup real maple syrup (or ⅓ cup honey)

juice from ½ lemon

dash each, cinnamon and nutmeg

½ pint heavy cream, whipped OR
1 cup yogurt

1 cup fresh fruit (coarsely shredded apples, sliced, fresh peaches, strawberries, pre-cooked and slightly-sweetened cranberries—you choose.)

Heat juice and syrup or honey to boiling. Sprinkle in the farina and cook slowly, constantly stirring, until thick and smooth. (about 8-10 minutes.) Pour into a large bowl and whip with wire whisk or electric beaters until light and fluffy (about 15 minutes). Fold in fresh fruit and whipped cream or yogurt. Chill.

Serve topped with fresh berries or chopped, toasted nuts.
Other possible garnishes: grated orange or lemon rind, an extra dusting of fresh-ground nutmeg,
a strawberry blossom.

Heavenly Compotes

(1) PEAR COMPOTE

serves 6-8

3 cups dried pears

½ cup maple syrup

1 cup water

dash of salt

2 cups heavy cream
(or yogurt)

Cook the pears, syrup and water together in a heavy saucepan. Simmer, uncovered, over very low heat until soft. Add salt. Pureé in a blender until smooth. Cool completely.

Whip the cream until fairly stiff. Fold the two together gently. Chill completely.
Optional: Fold in some <u>fresh</u> peach or pear slices before serving.

(2) APRICOT COMPOTE

serves 6-8

3 cups dried apricots

½ cup honey or maple syrup

1 cup water

dash of salt

2 cups yogurt or sour cream
(or a combination)

Cook the apricots and honey or syrup in water, same as above. Add salt; pureé and cool.

Fold in yogurt or sour cream.

Serve very cold.
Garnish with Fresh Fruit.

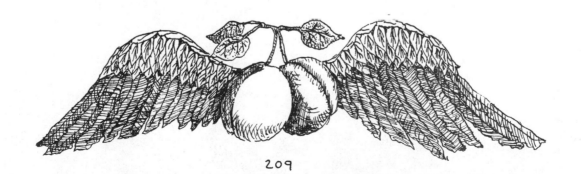

Ricotta-Almond Strudel

This recipe makes one large roll - enough for about six dessert servings or four brunch servings. Preparation time, including baking, comes to around an hour. The strüdel can be served hot or warm (brunch) or cold (dessert).

The Filling:

2 cups firm ricotta cheese, skim or whole

½ tsp. freshly-grated lemon rind

2 Tbs. fresh lemon juice

¼ - ⅓ cup honey (to taste)

¼ tsp. salt

¼ tsp. cinnamon

¼ cup chopped, toasted almonds

handful of raisins

2 eggs, beaten

½ cup fine breadcrumbs

¼ lb. melted butter (1 stick)

½ cup wheat germ

6 strudel leaves (cover with a damp cloth until ready to assemble.)

Combine all ingredients except butter, wheat germ and strudel leaves. Preheat oven to 375°.

Lay a leaf of strudel dough before you (use a clean wooden or formica surface), stretching out lengthwise away from you. Butter it liberally and gently, using a pastry brush. Sprinkle lightly with wheat germ. Add another strudel leaf and repeat the buttering and sprinkling and layering until all six leaves lie assembled before you in a neat pile.

Apply the filling here, and roll up, away from you, tucking in the sides.

Carefully lift the roll (use spatulas to help you, if necessary) and place it on a buttered tray. Brush the top with butter, and make several diagonal slashes, cutting (with serrated knife) through the top layer of dough to the filling. Bake 30-35 minutes - until golden and crisp. Cut it warm or cold, using a serrated knife and a gentle sawing motion.

Apple-Cheddar Strudel

preparation time,
including baking, about 1¼ hours   6 generous servings

Read through the recipe for
Ricotta-Almond Strudel (opposite)
-to get the general idea of this operation.

The Filling:

6 medium cooking apples

1 cup grated cheddar cheese

¼ lb. (1 stick) butter	½ cup honey	½ cup chopped walnuts
10 strudel leaves	1 tsp. cinnamon	rind and juice from 1 lemon
½ cup wheat germ	dash of salt	½ cup bread crumbs (fine)

optional: a handful of raisins

Combine all ingredients, except butter, strudel leaves and wheat germ. Heat oven to 375°. Assemble two rolls, using five leaves for each, being sure to brush butter between every two leaves. If desired, you can sprinkle extra wheat germ on top of the rolls.

Bake 30-35 minutes,
or until crisp
& brown.

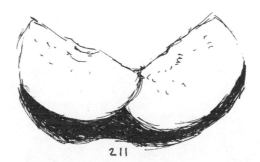

Serve warm or
cold,
with ice cream
or
whipped cream.

Crunchy-Top Peach Pie

Preheat oven to 400°.

one 9-incher

1 9" unbaked pie crust
1 egg yolk
} Brush crust with yolk. Let stand while you prepare the filling:

Toss peaches with flour and spices until they're evenly coated. Drizzle over the lemon juice and honey. Mix gently.
{ 4 heaping cups fresh, sliced peaches
2 Tbs. flour
juice from 1 large lemon
$\frac{1}{4}$ cup honey
$\frac{1}{2}$ tsp. cinnamon
couple of dashes of nutmeg

Let stand while you prepare the topping:

melted together {
2 cups raw rolled oats
5 Tbs. butter
3 Tbs. honey
$\frac{1}{2}$ tsp. cinnamon
$\frac{1}{2}$ cup chopped almonds
$\frac{1}{4}$ cup flour
$\frac{1}{2}$ tsp. salt
} Combine and mix well.

Pour peach filling into crust. Apply oat mixture evenly over peaches, and pat it firmly into place. Bake 35-45 minutes at 400° turned down to 375° after the first ten minutes. If the top browns too quickly, cover the pie with foil. Serve warm or cold.

Lemon Mousse

3 Tbs. cornstarch
½ cup confectioner's sugar
⅛ tsp. salt
½ cup fresh-squeezed lemon juice
½ cup water
2 eggs, separated
1 Tbs. light honey
1 tsp. freshly-grated lemon rind
½ pint heavy cream (cold)
1-2 Tbs. orange liqueur

(1) Sift together the cornstarch, sugar, and salt — into a small saucepan.

(2) Whisk the lemon juice and water into the sifted mixture. Cook, whisking constantly, over medium heat — until thick. (About 5 minutes.) Remove from heat.

(3) Beat the egg yolks in a medium-sized bowl. Drizzle a little (¼ cup) of the hot mixture into the beaten yolks (still beating), then return the yolks to the hot mixture, whisking constantly. Add honey. Return to heat and cook, stirring, over medium-low heat just 1 minute more. Remove from heat. Transfer to egg yolk bowl, and allow to cool to room temperature. (Stir it intermittently as it cools, to keep it smooth.)

(4) Beat egg whites until stiff. Fold into lemon mixture, along with lemon rind. Chill about 1 hour.

(5) Beat the heavy cream, with the liqueur, until stiff. Fold into the mousse. Chill at least 2 more hours before serving.

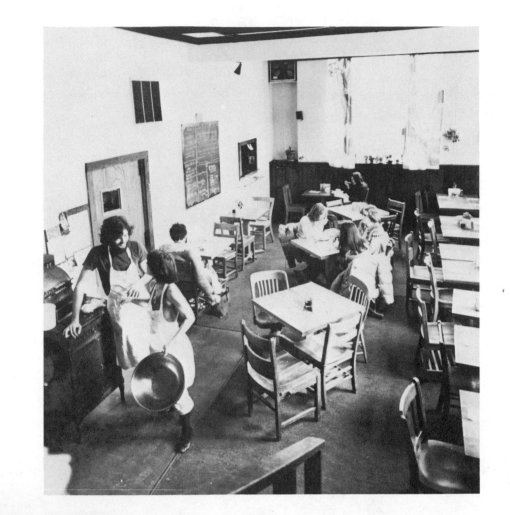

INDEX

THIS INDEX PROVIDES easy access to all recipes in this cookbook. Each recipe is indexed by main title, important ingredients, and often by the type of dish: for example, casseroles and nationality.

Achiote Seed
    in Salsa Yucateco 77
Aioli 71
ALMOND; ALMONDS:
    Apricot-Almond Bread 196
    Eggplant-Almond Enchiladas 156–157
    Ricotta-Almond Strudel 210
    Vegetable-Almond Medley 137
Alsatian Cheese Salad 53
Antipasto 60–61
APPLE; APPLES:
    Apple-Cheddar Strudel 211
    Apple-Cheese Pancakes 147
    Apple Chutney 73
    Apple-Honey Custard Pie 194
    Apple Krisp 186
    Cranapple-Walnut Cake 206

    in Bread Pudding 205; in Broiled Openfaced Sandwich 83; in Carrot-Yogurt Salad 55; in Cheese-Beans 154; in Chinese Duck Sauce 70; in crêpes 113; in Fruited Yogurt Desserts 191; in Fruit Soup 32; in Mushroom Curry 98; in Noodle Kugel 112; in Rice Pudding 193; in Stuffed Cabbage 109; in Stuffed Squash 128; in Waldorf Salad 56–57; in White Rabbit Salad 45
APRICOT; APRICOTS:
    Apricot Compote 209
    Apricot-Almond Bread 196
Arabian Squash-Cheese Casserole 134
ARTICHOKES:
    marinated for Antipasto 61
    stuffed 102
ASPARAGUS:
    Asparagus-Mushroom Sauce 67
    Cream of Asparagus Soup 3
    in crêpes 113
AVOCADOS: in Guacamole 94; in salad dressing 41; in Tostada 144; in Waldorf Salad 41

Baba Ganouj, 92–3
Baked Maple-Egg Custard, 197
Baked things at Moosewood, 173–74
BANANA; BANANAS:
    Banana Bread 189
    Banana Raita 72
    Banana-Sour Cream Pie 203
BARLEY: in Mushroom-Barley Soup 25
BASIL: in Pesto 74
Bavarian-style sandwich, 87
BEANS:
  BLACK:
    Brazilian Black Bean Soup 26
  FRESH GREEN:
    Bermuda Salad 59
    Vegetable-Walnut Pâté 90

    in crêpes 113; in Gado Gado 104; in Gypsy Soup 5; in Multi-Bean Salad 54; in Summer Vegetable Soup 15; in Tempura and Pakora 152–53
  GARBANZO ("CHICK PEAS"):
    Antipasto 60
    Felafel 140
    Gypsy Soup 5
    Humus 91
    Minestrone Soup 7
  KIDNEY:
    Cheese-Beans 154
    Vegetarian Chili 110
  LIMA:
    Succotash Chowder 10
  NAVY (also "WHITE PEA"):
    Minestrone Soup 7
    White Bean and Black Olive Soup 22
  PINTO:
    Cheese-Beans 154
    Refritos 143
BEET; BEETS:
    Chilled Buttermilk-Beet Borscht 38
    Russian Cabbage Borscht 27
    "Colorful Accompaniment" 129

    in Bleu Cheese Sandwich 89; in Fresh Vegetable Salad 41

Special thanks to
⊁Mary A. Ochs⊀
for her work on this index.

PLEASE SEND
FEEDBACK TO :

Mollie Katzen
c/o Ten Speed Press
P.O. Box 7123
Berkeley, Ca. 94707

Notes

Notes

Notes

... and here come 250 *more* original vegetarian recipes, including a whole chapter on breads, in addition to soups (hot and chilled), salads, many entrees, light meals for nibblers, dips, desserts, menu-planning ideas, and guidelines for improvisation, by Mollie Katzen:

The Enchanted Broccoli Forest

...and other timeless delicacies

by Mollie Katzen

author of the Moosewood Cookbook

8½ × 11 inches   320 pages   Indexed
Handlettered/Illustrated Throughout
Paper, $11.95   Cloth, $16.95